LETTERS
FROM
IRISH COLLEGE

First published in 1996 by
Marino Books
An imprint of Mercier Press
16 Hume Street Dublin 2

Trade enquiries to Mercier Press
PO Box 5, 5 French Church Street, Cork

A Marino Original

© the contributors 1996
© introduction Rose Doyle 1996

ISBN 1 86023 036 9

10 9 8 7 6 5 4 3 2 1

A CIP record for this title is available
from the British Library

Cover design by Cathy Dineen
Set by Richard Parfrey
Printed in Ireland by ColourBooks,
Baldoyle Industrial Estate, Dublin 13

LETTERS
FROM
IRISH COLLEGE

EDITED BY ROSE DOYLE

Fionnuala Brennan's photographs: Loughanure 1960 and Gweedore 1961

O'Donnell family photograph Ring 1963

O'Donnell family photograph Ballybunion 1966

O'Donnell family photograph Ballybunion 1966

CONTENTS

INTRODUCTION

Other cultures have camps, schools and activity centres for their young to play and grow up in during the summer months. We have the Gaeltacht.

Unique and wholly homegrown, the Gaeltacht colleges have been a rite of passage for hundreds of thousands of Irish youngsters since the state itself was a stripling. The Gaeltacht is where girls meet boys and boys girls for the first time away from their parents. The agonies of homesickness strike first at the Gaeltacht and it's also where, recovered from homesickness, youngsters enjoy their first, heady savourings of freedom and independence. Friends are made for life at the Gaeltacht, hearts are broken, the value of money is first appreciated and young palates begin to discover that hunger is good sauce. And it all, of course, happens *as Gaeilge*.

Getting these letters together opened a floodgate. There were those who'd rather forget (but can't) and those who never will, those who wrote letters every day and those, like Tánaiste Dick Spring, who hadn't time to write any.

Not everyone's letters, alas, were kept. Memories are another thing. Poignant, bitter, happy, sometimes sad, they are *always* vivid.

Mary Banotti MEP shuddered when asked for a letter. She was a teenager with Leaving Cert looming when she was sent to Carraigaholt in the late 1950s.

Her account was full of words like 'desperate',

'miserable' and 'bleak'. Her abiding memories are of 'the outside lavatory, the cold and the newspaper we had to use there.' And her abiding impression was that Gaeltacht people felt it a duty to put manners on the spoilt, middle-class English-speaking city children who arrived in their midst.

Film producer Michael O'Herlihy, on the other hand, said cheerfully of his year in Ring that he 'went there a boy and came home a man.' He says too that he carried the Gaeltacht experience with him throughout a thirty-nine year career in Hollywood.

O'Herlihy's Gaeltacht tale comes from another Ireland and is a dramatic illustration of how things have changed. He tells of arriving in Ring on 1 September 1939, 'the day the war broke out.' He was ten years old, 'a little brat,' and Ring was, he says, 'quite a Dickensian set-up.' In bleak midwinter it was 'bitter, cold and damp' with the only heating from open fires. The menu varied between porridge, white bread, tea and 'all sorts of strange potatoes'. He was regularly 'beaten black and blue' – once with a hot poker – and, as a Dubliner, had his 'first contact with racism'. He's had a theory ever since that 'Auschwitz got the book of rules from Ring.'

But he's never regretted that year. 'One of the best things ever happened to me was going to Ring,' he says. 'I had to fend for myself and I won in the long run. It was a year well spent.' He remembers the *Fear Mór,* who was 6'8" and ran the college. And he remembers the 'second head', Micheal O'Donnell, taking them for walks along the beaches and on Helvick Head. 'He was a lovely man, very enlightened, and if you'd been good he'd let you shoot at rabbits. It was there I learned to shoot . . . '

He learned Irish too. 'I was very proud of my Irish when I left. I visited a few years ago and to my horror they don't have a *Fear Mór* any longer. They have a manager.'

Dr Garret FitzGerald is another alumnus of Coláiste na Rinne. He spent all the school year 1935–36 there and returned for the Easters of 1938, 1939 and 1940. A letter in Irish, written to his father in London just after he came home from the year in Ring, bears testimony to the thoroughness of the Ring teaching methods. It is also testimony to Dr FitzGerald's own searching intelligence as a ten-year-old that he included in his letter some lines in the Quichua language of the Incas of Peru.

From what was going to be a fairly straightforward, whimsical collection, these letters have grown to become almost a slice of social history.

On money there is Dr FitzGerald again, this time in 1938, writing about his 3/3 return bus ticket from Dungarvan to Waterford. Journalist Colm Keane, in a postcard in 1963, is anguished at paying 7/- return from Cork to Ballingeary. In the great leaps and changes between then and 1995 the cost of sending a *bike* to Tralee from Dublin rose to £17.50.

And there's behaviour. In 1961 sixteen years old Fionnuala Brennan wrote to her mother that she was going to 8 am mass 'almost every day' and that she'd got ink spilled on her dress and had got off school to wash it.

Thirty-four years later, in 1995, Susan Murray wrote jokily to her mother that she was 'learning lots of Irish

13

and smoking lots of hash and drinking (*not*). So whatever you do, Mom, don't come down . . . '

But some things never change. Complaints about food are legion and run through letters from every decade. Moans about stew and jelly and cold, lumpy custard are bettered only by tales of flushing it all down the loo.

No one ever had enough money, everyone loved the *céilís* and most people, initially, hated the people they shared rooms with – people who later became friends for life.

And the *cri de coeur* of homesickness is, of course, a seam running through. It's at its most heartbreaking in a 1986 letter from thirteen-year-old Conor McManamly. 'All I want to do is *go home!*' he writes, 'please, please, please take me home . . . the pain . . . I can't stand it any longer . . .' Just five days later he'd recovered enough to write: 'things have completely changed like you said they would . . . '

Girls suffer too. Jane Kelly, in 1994, was so trauma-tised that that she promised to 'go without new clothes for the rest of my childhood' and to get out her *Jimín* and teach herself Irish. She went home but she survived.

They all did. These are their letters. Enjoy them as much as I did.

Publishers' note
No attempt has been made to 'correct' or impose uniformity of spelling on the letters in this collection, whether they are in Irish or in English. Only the punctuation of dates, salutations and addresses has been made standard.

LETTERS 1936–1995

From: *Garret Fitzgerald*
Age: *10*
Year: *1936*
Home: *Bray, County Wicklow*
Gaeltacht: *Ring, County Waterford*

Colaiste na Rinne
Dúngarbhán
Saturday, 7 March 1936

A athair dhílis

I hope you are well and that Uncle William is getting better. Mother wrote me and said he was ill and that you had gone over to see him. This short, humble letter is to Auntie Katie and Auntie Sissie, Uncle Edward, Uncle France and Uncle William himself as well as you and Ulick and Gerald can look at it.

Give Uncle William my special love and tell him I hope to see him next summer.

With lots of love	(*le grá mór*)
from	(*ó*)
Garret	(*Gearóid*)

PS Mother will give you the news.
PPS I forgot Jem and Kay. Give them my love. G. F.

Cnuc na Side
Bri Cualainn
22 July 1936

A athair dhílis

Tá an-áthas orm go bhfuil tú go maith agus go maith leat an teas.

Tháinig Deasmún ar maidin dé Satharn. Bhíos i mBlá Cliath inde agus chuadas go dtí an Seodhlann ann. An ceann leis na stampaí agus rudaí óir ann.

Ag a dó a chlog do dúisig Maimí mé aréir cun go bhfeicfheadh mé an réal nuadh.

Tá sé 11 am anois agus níl éinne ach mé féin agus Maimí éirighthe. Tá cúpla buacaillí on Rínn ag teacht anseo inniu. Bhíodar anseo cúpla uaire cheana féin. Tá brón orm nach bhfuil tusa anseo mar bímís a' cainnt Gaedhlachg i gcómhnuidhe.

Cheannaigh Maimí liathróid criocar Spáinneac indé.

Beunos días, mi padre, cómo está, muy bien. Adios.

Good morning, my father. How are you? I am well. Good-bye.

Quichua.

Cani pi ocapana. Pura acarhuay. Ach acahuara. Achallay.

I am in the sunset.

Rinn. 1938/39
5.30 (winter time)

[This letter begins on page 3; the rest has been mislaid.]

18

We had to stop for a long time at Kilkenny and Ballyhale to fix up the cattle again and we got to Waterford at 2.25 pm (an hour and five minutes late).

I had to run and the bag wasn't too light either. It's a good walk – or rather run – from the station to the bus stop and you can imagine what I felt like when I arrived just in time to catch no interchange tickets! I got to Dungarvan but as the *Fear Mór* was in America he didn't meet me. I went to the garage and as usual when I arrive they were all at a funeral. I waited for half an hour and managed to get one for 6/- leaving me with 3/3 return bus ticket to Waterford and the train ticket and 5/- pocket money and 10/- extra. I got to Ring and did not succeed in making any friends for half an hour. Then I met a boy who came last week and I've had great sport ever since.

Lots of love from your loving son

Garret

PS I've got my bed.

From:	*Seamus Ó Riain*
Age:	*9*
Year:	*1940*
Home:	*Delgany, County Wicklow*
Gaeltacht:	*Ring, County Waterford*

11 August 1940

Dear Mammy and Daddy

I want to stay longer. Aunty Nelly and I may stay till

Saturday or Sunday (and I am staying). But I wonder could Brian stay at home for a bit. Thanks for the parcel. Please write and let me know.

Best love from

Séamus Ó Riain

22 July 1941

Dear Mammy and Daddy

I got your parcel yesterday and was delighted with it especially with the shirt even do I dident wear it yet. Pierce has not got his holidays yet, he might be getting them this week or next week, then he will come back with us in the car when it comes down in about two weeks at the least. Brian will be coming up to spend one night and then go into town with Daddy to the train next morning, so may Martin come as well as Pierce?

Love to all

Séamus Ó Riain

From: Ann Farrell
Age: 8
Year: 1953
Home: Dublin
Gaeltacht: Ring, County Waterford

[From Ann Farrell, who was on holiday near Ring, County Waterford, with her mother and others in the family. Her brothers were nearby in Ring College. In 1953 she wrote to

her father, working at home in Dublin.]

Dear Daddy

I hope you are well. And I hope you got the letter and will you send me a letter on Monday?

I hope the apples will be ripe when we get home. And I hope you are getting your dinner well and Marie [her younger sister] is not eating well yet and Jim [younger brother] did not wet the bed yet. And Mammy is not eating well. And Mammy has a pain in her throat. And we are getting on well.

Last night myself and the girls went out with Mrs Rapple and Bertie to a farm way out in the country and we had a great time everywhere we went. And the boys are going out with Bertie.

Again don't forget to send the letter.

Love from

Ann and all

Ring

[1953]

Dear Daddy

I hope you are well. And you didn't send me the letter and we are going to the pictures tonight with Paddy and Tomás and the rest of the boys and girls. And Mammy went to the pictures with Mrs O'Brien on Thursday night. And Mammy's mouth is not better yet and she is not eating well yet. We have a lot more people down here now so the place is pretty full. More girls came so we have plenty to play with and no more boys came down yet but we don't mind. And Jim had a great time with the pigs and calves and we all helped Mrs Rapple milk the cows.

And don't forget to send me the letter. And Daddy I reminded you to send me that letter and I will not remind you again and I hope everyone on the road is well. And you were supposed to send a letter on Monday.
Best love from
Ann

Dear Daddy
I got your letter alright. I am getting a sore mouth like Mammy and Daddy tell Catherine [a friend] that I will be home on Saturday, please God. And I sent a card to Catherine and Barbara and Margaret. And Daddy I like down here very much and I hope you don't miss us. And Marie is in for a swim every morning, she is great in the water. And Mammy did not get in for a swim she said she would get in for a swim before the end of the week, please God.

And Daddy I hope you will send me another letter before the end of the week. We went for a walk on Monday. We don't like going home.
Best love from
Ann

_____

From: *Fionnuala Brennan*
Age: *15*
Year: *1960/1961*
Home: *Belfast*
Gaeltachts: *Loughanure/Gweedore County Donegal*

Loch an Iubhar
near Rannafast
County Donegal
Summer 1960

Dear Mother

The bus from Strabane took a long time and when we arrived here it was raining and there was a wind. There are eight of us in a room. The priest came and said we had to move. I was mad because Dot and I were in the same house and wanted to stay together. But I was moved anyway and now there are four of us to a room, sharing two double beds. The room is so small and there is so little space that we can't all get up together. We get up one by one, waiting until the other is dressed and leaves. There are no wardrobes so we hang our clothes on the back of the door. The *bean an tí* and the *fear* sleep on a settle bed beside the fire. There is no bathroom except for a '*teach beag*' at the end of the garden at the back of the house. We get bacon and cabbage *every day* and on Sundays we get it too except that then we get carrigeen moss as a dessert with it.

I don't like Loch an Iubhar. There are nine boys and eleven girls in my class. We got to Mass every day at 8.30 am and we're in school at 10.30 am. Everyone has to go to

23

Mass. The *caeli* was no good and I was sitting in a corner all night long. The good thing is that I am learning to swim.

It is *ag cur go trom* outside now. Please write to me.
With love from
Fionnuala

Rannafast

County Donegal

Dear Mother

I really like it here now, though I haven't been at Mass for two days. I am getting awfully lazy. We are all beginning to feel sad now about going home.

It is raining practically every day and we play cards a lot. We do other things too. In Rannafast the other day we listened to the juke box until 5 o'clock. The priest gave us a lift back. I am going to see *Mise Éire* tonight and am really looking forward to it. Pat and I were given permission to go to Rannafast on our own and we toured the whole place and walked seventeen miles. It was terrific.

The play that myself and some of the others were rehearsing so hard won first prize. We were delighted!

We will be packing to go in a couple of days and some people are crying already at the idea. The last *ceile mór* will last from 11 pm to 2 am, which is terrific. Most of us will be going through Letterkenny to Strabane and we have promised ourselves that we will sing on the bus all the way home.
With love from
Fionnuala

Gweedore
1 August [1961]

Dear Mother

I love this place. The scenery is lovely and the house I'm in is very nice. I'm glad I'm not in the other house. There's a big fuss made of everything there.

The first *caeli* I went to this year I was *rushed!* But I didn't go the next night because there is no really interesting talent. Things are a bit strict sometimes. For instance we went to the beach and sat on a boat and the parish priest came and told us we weren't allowed. We go to 8 am Mass almost every day.

By the way, I got ink spilled on my dress but it's all right. I got off school to wash it. It was raining and we sat around the fire and told stories.

Thank you for the money.

With love from

Fionnuala

Gweedore
[1961]

Dear Mother

Everything is fine here except that I am fed up with school. The other day ten of us decided to go to Falcarragh. We hitched good lifts there and had a good time watching Brendan Behan and Anew McMaster. But my lungs don't feel too good so I'm going to give up smoking (joke!).

The crowd here are brilliant and we're all feeling a bit

sad about the end of things. We get a half day from school the day we leave and the Dublin boys have promised to help us with our bags.

With love from

Fionnuala

From: *Colm Keane*
Age: *10*
Year: *1963*
Home: *Cork*
Gaeltacht: *Ballingeary, County Cork (Coláiste na Mumhan)*

[Six postcards]

Dear Mam and Dad

I am having a great time here, I have only 2/6 left because I paid 7/- return from Cork to Ballingeary, 5/- return Youghal to Cork, 2/6 for a book, schoolbooks 4/- and that leaves 16/6 and I don't know how I spent it. Send on my racket.

Love

Colm

Dear Mam and Dad

Enjoying my stay. Woman of the house is very cross. Still have pound. See you in a month.

Colm

Dear Mam and Dad

I am having a good time.The *ceili* are a laugh. I am in the junior class and I have not hard Irish. Please send on my tennis racket, they have one hard court here. It is not much good but it will do. There are nice boys in my room. I sleep in a single bed.

Bye for now

Colm

Dear Mam

When I was coming from Cork to Ballingeary I bought a 7/- return ticket and when I got here I put it in my wallet and then I put it in my case. Yesterday I looked in my case and it was gone. That means it was stolen. Other boys had same keys. That cost me 3/6.

Love

Colm

Dear Mam

I am having a great time here. I will phone you some time soon. I am getting hungrier every minute of the day. Imagine I am here a week now, it flew didn't it. We got a very small piece of steak the other day, it was terrible. Send on food. That is an SOS. Some cold ham as well. Write soon.

Colm

Dear Mam

Thanks for the food. It was lovely. On Monday send me on three pkts of biscuits, four small 4d cakes, one pkt cheese, some sweets and six of the 1d bars, also send on

5/-. I don't want my suit pants. Don't forget please.
Love
Colm

From: Sheila O'Donnell
Age: 11
Year: 1964
Home :   Dublin
Gaeltacht: Gortahork, County Donegal/ Coláiste Bhréan-
               ainn, Ballybunion, County Kerry

Coláiste Uladh
Gorta horc
County Donegal
8 July

Dear Mummy and Daddy,

I hope all the family are well. I got Daddy's letter on
Monday and the others on Tuesday thanks for the letters
and money and stamps, I gave Rory half them.

I have bought Rory a tiny penknife and corkscrew in
the shape of a bottle for his birthday. Deirdre and myself
went out to the beach with the Fitzgeralds today. (Lucia's
mother and father they are staying in a hotel in Gweedore.)
We had our tea in the hotel. After tea we went to the shops
and got ice-cream and chocolate we were back when the
ceili was just over so we two missed it.

Deirdre and myself both have boyfriends don't tell
anyone especially the girls.

Deirdre got hers first he gave her a ring. then I got mine he gave me a ring it is lovely.

I don't think I have any more news give my love to Anne and Eoin and thank Anne for the letter.

Love

Sheila xoxoxoxox

Coláiste Uladh
Gort Ahorc
Litter Kenny
County Donegal
13 July 1964

Dear Mummy and Daddy

I hope all the family are well. Rory got the parcel and card and letter. He was meant to give me the skirt on Saturday but he didn't give it to me till today. He forgot to, it is lovely I got the socks and I was very glad to because two of my pairs were wet and my other one was dirty.

Please send us money for the tour it is 8/6 each the tour is on on Sunday next we are to have our money for it as soon as possible can we have some money to spend on the tour.

Please send us some sweets as you can not get very good ones here and they are very dear (at least most of them are).

An inspector came the other day he did not ask me any questions he was very nice.

My boy-friend was sick to-night so I did not have many dances at the *ceilí*. I wore my skirt to the *ceilí*. We went to

29

the park to-day it is a field we play in it has lots of rushes in it we make St Brigids crosses from them to-day we were playing red-rover, relay races and netball. I was not playing netball I was making crosses with a few other people while the others were playing.

My togs dry very quickly. When I came out of the water after my last swim, they were nearly dry. I am sorry for not writing sooner but we have not much free time all the letters I have written so far were written in bed including this one. I can't think of any thing to write.

We are having a wonderful time here. That's all for now.

Love

Sheila xoxoxox

PS Give my love to Anne and Eoin.

PS We got your letter today 14th thanks for the money and stamps and of course the letter. The Tour is 8/6 not 7/6. I have paid the extra shilling from my pocket money. I am rushing this as I have to go to school. Goodbye for now.

Sheila xoxox

Coláiste Uladh
Gorta horc
Litter Kenny
County Donegal

Dear Mum and Dad
I hope you are all well.

Rory gave me a letter to send to you but I lost it so I have to tell you all the news here. Do not tell him I lost it or he would be furious. This is what he wrote as far as I can remember.

Dear Mum and Dad
    I hope you are all well.
    I have some bad news for you I have lost my return (bike) bycycle ticket. Would you please send me 10/- to buy a new one at Derry. With it send us four shillings each for our bikes on the bus. (he wrote a few more things like the weather here is not good and so on) then he wrote PS give my love to Anne and Eoin xoxoxoxoxoxox
Love
Rory

    Please send us a parcel of sweets. Everyone gets them and money goes very quickly here. I have none left. I hope you are all well.
Love
Sheila
PS Don't forget to send Rory's 10/- for his bike.

Gort-a-horc
Litter Kenny
County Donegal

Dear Eoin and Anne
    I hope you are keeping well.
    Would you please tell Mummy that we have no money left and ask her to send us some to spend on the tour on Sunday. Money goes very quickly here.

A girl in my class got a huge parcel to day. She couldn't wait to get home to open it, there was a dress, a jumper, sweets and comics in it. She told me in school this afternoon.

I am still getting short of money, so would you send 5/- down for a *fáinne* as I won't have enough money for that myself.

Please send my skirt and blouse down if they're ready. I don't mind really if you don't send them but would you send a bit of tuck for the last night as we are having another midnight feast as it will be a girls's birthday. Sorry for asking you for so many things.

We are having a great time here the water is always lovely and the waves are enormous.

The other night our class had the play Cinderella. There were two fairies coming with the fairy godmother. I was one of them and all went well in the rehersals but in the real thing when the fairy godmother came in she slipped and fell flat on her face, we were all in fits and couldn't keep the laughing in, but the rest of the play went all right.

Rory dances with Mary Styles a lot at the *céilís*.

Yesterday the sea was lovely and the waves were enormous. We had a great swim and after it we were able to sunbathe in our togs as it was the first warm day we have had, the rest of the days have been windy or wet or cold.

That's all the news I have, how is Eoin and yourself. We're having a great time.

Bye for now.

Love
Sheila xxxxxxxxxx

PS Don't forget to send the forms back signed as soon as possible.

Coláiste Bhréanainn
Baile an Buineána
County Kerry
Friday-Saturday

Dear Mummy and Daddy

I hope you are well we are very well here.

I am in Rang 3. So are Mary and Marion and Bessie and her friend Patricia. Bairbre is in Rang 2 and so is Rory. I am in a different room to Bairbre but I am in the same room as Bessie and Mary nad Marion and Bessie's friend.

We arrived here at about ten to nine and went straight to the *céilí* and we went to bed at about 10.30.

We didn't have mass this morning so we didn't have to get up till 8.30.

We have just had our dinner it was awful, it was fish (coated in pepper) and mashed potatoes and cabbage and for sweet we had cold rice, it was awful. The breakfast was not bad. We only had two classes this morning but we usually have three.

We had a swim this afternoon the water was lovely and the waves were enormous. Mary Styles sprained her ankle at the beach and she couldn't go to the *ceili* to-night and probably won't be going to the beach to-day. We are having a great time here. That's all the news I have now.

Love

Sheila

PS You needn't send my dressing gown but will you send my navy polo neck with my skirt and blouse if you can.
Sheila

Coláiste Bhréanainn
Ballybunion
County Kerry
29 June

Dear Mummy and Daddy

I hope you and Eoin are well. We arrived here at 3.30 yesterday but we had to wait till after tea to get our beds and then when we had unpacked we had a *céilí* so I couldn't write to you.

They are very strict here about speaking Irish.

Anne and I are in a dorm with eight bunks and one bed. Anne is on the top bunk and I am on the bottom. In a few minutes we are going to have an oral exam to find what class we're in (I'm dreading it).

In our class there is nine girls, seven of them are called Maire and one girl called Finola and there is also nine boys in our class, Rory is one of them, he sits behind me. Catherine and Anne are in the class higher than me.

We had a great swim this afternoon. The waves were fabulous, and the water was lovely. We go for a swim every day.

The first night Catherine's room were caught speaking English and were told that if they did anything else they would be sent home, but last night they had a midnight feast and they were not caught.

There is a tuck shop here it does not sell very much but at the end of the month things go down to half price so our room are having a feast then. I have no more news so goodbye for now.

Love

Sheila

Coláiste Bhréanainn

Bally Bunion

County Kerry

Dear Mum and Dad

Sorry for not writing sooner but I had a letter written and I lost it. Rory will kill me for not sending his letter yet so don't tell him that I'm only sending it now.

How are you and Eoin? We are very well here. The food is much better than it was last year.

Uncle Tom and Bessie came down to see us on Sunday. They didn't know it was Rory's birthday but when they found out they gave him a ball and they gave us 10/- each and some sweets. They took us to tea in the west end.

I am sorry for asking you to ask Mummy for so many things but I forgot to ask in my letter to them just one more thing. I will have no more envelopes after this one and not much notepaper. I am just after going to the shop for some girls out of our room and when I came back Deirdre had taken two pages of my pad. She's awfully mean and she has had more of my envelopes than myself. She took most of them and she said she would be buying more. I am not talking to her but when *bean an tí* came in she was real quiet and talked really quietly and sounded sick.

I can't think of any more news.

Goodbye for now.

Love

Sheila xoxoxoxoxoxoxoxoxoxo

Coláiste Bhréana

Ballybunion

County Kerry

6 July

Dear Mum and Dad and Eoin

I hope you and Eoin are well. We are very well, the food is not very nice but all right. We got your parcel thanks for it and for letting us keep the whole five pounds between us.

Please send on my flipflops because I need them for walking to the beach. We go to the beach every day, Yesterday it was wet and we were not going to go, but we did, and there were curraghs there, it was lovely, ('it' means the water) the waves are very big here they are much bigger than the waves in Kilkee maybe I'm just imagining it because I'm used to them but I don't find them that big any more.

Rory got his parcel just now thanks for the tube, (we got our letter too, thanks for it). Rory has not opened the parcel yet he's not allowed to open it till he goes into the dorm.

This is the evening now we had great fun this afternoon, first of all we had relay races, one team of girls and one team of boys. There were four chairs two at each end of the room, on the two at the top there was two pennies one on each chair. You had to run up and around the top chair and while you were going around you had to pick up the penny and down around the other chair and up again, it was great fun.

Thanks again for the tube (although I can swim a few strokes). That's all for the present.

Love

Sheila xoxoxoxoxoxoxo

From: *Anne O'Donnell*
Age: *11/14*
Year: *1963–4/1966*
Home: *Dublin*
Gaeltacht: *Ring, County Waterford/Coláiste Bhréanainn, Ballybunion, County Kerry*

Coláiste na Rinne
Dúngarbhán
County Portláirge
20 September 1963

Dear Mummy and Daddy

I hope you and all the family are well. We have started playing camoige here and it is great fun we play it every evening before and after study.

We were going swiming for a while as the beach is just down the steps at the back of the college, but when the good weather broke we were all disipionted.

37

Thank you very much for the parcel and the letter and cards as I got two from Daddy one in the morning and one in the evening on Wednesday, would you please send me some more Halliborange pills, my music books, some fruit, and a fine-comb. What I mean by a fine-comb is one of those dandruf combs which we have at home the brand we need is called 'Black Elephant' as the fine comb has reminded me would you please send me on about three hair bands it does not matter what sort they are the reason I need them is because my red one is very dirty.

Nidge and I are very well and we are having a great time playing and going for walks we go for a walk every day but I cannot go as I have to practice music from quarter past four to half past four. I hope I havent asked for too much.

Lots of love

Anne xxxxxxx

Coláiste na Rinne
Dúngarbhán
County Portláirge
13 April 1964

Dear Sheila

This is just a line to know how you are. All's well here.

We went on a very long walk last Sunday and some people said they had blisters on their feet.

We had the Doctrine exam yesterday and everybody got easy quotations, the priest was very nice.

There is going to be a tennis competion in the middle of the term and everybody is practicing very hard.

The weather here is quite good but it is raining today.

Give my love to the boys and Ros and the rest.

Lots of love

Anne xoxoxoxo

PS Would you please send me on some tuck as I only have two oranges left. The slip was a little bit too long but I took it up in the shoulders as you said.

Thats all for now.

Lots of love

Anne xoxoxox

PS Please send me on some Villesion as I have none left.

> Coláiste Breannainn
> Bally Bunion
> County Kerry

Dear Mum, Dad and Eoin

I hope ye are all well. We are well enough this place is OK exept for the food ugh. It is awful.

We got your letter and the parcel you sent Rory.

Monica and Michael are staying here in Bally Bunion and they brought us out today and they are also bringing us out on Friday.

My boyfriend's name is Willie O'Sullivan he is a scream. He lives in Limerick and his father owns a shop and a public house in Limerick town. He goes to Sexton Street school.

The tuck shop here is well stocked up but it is awfully hard not to spend money as it is so near you that every time you are hungry you simply have to go and spend something.

Would you please send me on a biro and my autograph book. Would you also send on a long sleeved blouse one of the white school ones size 8 or 7–8 if possible.

We have been for lots of swims, every day exept for one which was wet.

The *céilís* are terific fun.

That's all for now.

Anne

xoxoxoxox

From: Eoin O'Donnell
Age: 13
Year: 1970
Home: Dublin
Gaeltacht: Coláiste Bhréanainn, Ballybunion, County Kerry

Coláiste Brendaín
Sandhill Road
Ballybunion
County Kerry

Dear Mum and Dad

Having an OK time the food is pretty shite and the gravy is greasy water. A lot of things have happened since you visited me, two boys put aspros in coke and got drunk yesterday which was Monday. There was a watch stolen this morning from a boys case. On Saturdays we go to confession in town and we are allowed to go into a shop across the road from the church, but everything is very dear in that shop.

Seamus let me go into another shop on the way home. This is our daily routine 8.00 oclock we get up, we have Mass at 8.15, after Mass we have breakfast and after breakfast we have an hour free time, then we have class which begins at 10.00 and ends at 1.00, then we have dinner. Then I usually play tennis or clock golf till about 4.00, then we go to the beach till half past five then we come home for tea then we have prayers after about an hour of a break then cleascaddle or splash-paddle as we call it then we have the *céilí* untill 11.00 then we go to bed. The weather is lousy rain every day or else fog or else its sultry. We are always tired and it is getting monotonous going to the *céili* every night we all think four or five *céilis* is enough for a week. I was playing football for the first time yesterday. Monday but we lost 3-6 to 2-8 and naturally enough I didn't score because I was a back and because I couldn't score even if I was a forward. Still I enjoyed the game and thats the main thing I suppose. No-one has been sent home yet but I dont suppose anyone will be sent home. I hope not. I have a lot of freinds here we met three boys from Newbridge. Their names are Bill Mulvey, Tom Shaw and Rory O'Donnell. We had a pillow-fight last night against the other dormitory and we were caught by Brian. We have started to play soccer on the beach, but we pick the ball up when one of the teachers are around. There is a robber in the college and we think we know who it is. We are going to be allowed into one of the amusement casinos but the one they are going to let us go to has no slot machines. I am glad because they are a waste of money, but there are dodgems and all the things they used to have in Killkee. We are planing to have a midnight feast on the last night and we found some candles on the beach which we intend to use as lights for the feast. I was given some sort of docet which I dont know what to do with that seems to be all there is to say.

Love

Eoin

From:	*Anthony Deegan*
Age:	*16*
Year:	*1966*
Home:	*Dublin*
Gaeltacht:	*Ballingeary, County Cork (Coláiste na Mumhan)*

An Óstán

Coláiste Na Mumhan

Ballingeary

County Cork

Tuesday 2 August 1966

Dear Mary

Weather fantastic, only one thing about it though. It hasn't stopped raining since we came. There's nothing to do, only look out the window at it and pray that it will stop before we go home but looking at it now I don't think it will. It's driving me mad.

We had great fun coming down on the train, I don't know what we did that made it so good though, for a start there was about fourteen in a compartment which was made to hold six that's what I call comfort. O yes and another thing, I met some woman at the station, who's little son was coming here and she asked me to look after him, of course I said I would. That's where I put my big foot in it, he has turned out the biggest pup you could ever meet, he's driving me up the wall. But seeing that he makes my bed polishes my shoes and gives me sweets I think I just may be able to stand him.

Last night and this morning was also a great laugh. Last night we didn't sleep at wink of course, Colgan couldn't sleep with cramp so he wouldn't let anyone else sleep. It's just my luck to be sleeping on top of him, well not on top of him! above him, we're in bunks. So seeing that we couldn't sleep a few of us got up to have a pillow fight. It didn't last long, as far as I was concerned though the first swing I made at a fellow I pulled something in my back, its still at me I hope its not a slipped disc, just my luck. Well at about twenty to six this morning, when we knew for sure that we weren't going to get any sleep, four of us got up for a game of tennis, the mist was so thick we could hardly see the ball, about a half an hour later Colgan and Gillen got up so we jacked up the game, went up the road a bit and knocked off five bicycles (Gillan didn't come) and went out the road about two miles to where the girls stay. Well to say the least of it we woke them up. We then came back, returned the bicycles, this was about half seven. We then plonked ourselves down on the road and had a fag, good job no cows came, or we were dead. (At this stage I'm wondering will you be even able to read this I write so small and I'm trying to write on the top of a bunk also that Pat is jumping all over the place, the little F . . . r) I hope you can though). You know the old saying 'Try try and try again if at first you don't succeed try try and try again.' I think its appropriate in this case.

Well that's all the excitement we have had so far of course the *céilí* has to come yet. I just can't wait for it, I wonder what group will be playing, there's talk of the Stones being here tonight but, I don't believe it. What was the No. 5 like (that kid is back) Monday night? (*Help!*) What did Mary think of it? I hope you enjoyed yourselves.

Well that's all I can say for now, except could you please send me a photograph of yourself, to keep up the old spirit you know, please.

Love Tony xxxxxxxx

PS Write soon (O no its back)

An Óstán
Coláiste na Murnhan
Ballingeary
County Cork
August 1966

My dear Mary

Received your letter yesterday and thanks much. The weather hasn't improved much since I last wrote to you, yesterday it was so bad that we couldn't even go to Mass, at least we refused to go and they couldn't make us. You said you hoped Michael was better, I don't know what I said was wrong with him, but the two of us were at the doctor this morning with sprained fingers, he got his playing basketball and I got mine playing hurling. It was great fun at the doctor though and we got off school all morning. Speaking of school we have mitched three times so far, not bad. The other day Mick two others and I were going to mitch and an old mad farmer got us. We ran.

Life could be better could be worse here, thats the only way I can put it, we have quite a bit of fun but the rest of the time is just misery. Last Sunday we all went out to Gougan Barra. Most of them walked but three of us just sat on the road and waited for someone to stop for us. After about two hours, who stopped but the PP. One of the lads had a guitar and we had to sing Irish songs for him. We were singing '*An poc ar buile*' and I forgot myself and shouted out 'I'll fucken kill you'. Judging by the look he gave me I'd say he didn't like it. There's no swimming allowed out there so Gillen and I went out (sorry in) in our jeans it was great but was awful walking home 'Oh stop it'. I'm confirmed we are mad. Then on Monday some nut suggested that we should go to school in our P.J.'s (pyjamas) so we did, only in the tops of course. Sully never got as far as the school though, he was just going out of the *Óstán* when the master noticed that they were P.J.'s and sent him back.

I was made captain of a football, hurling and basketball team and it's bloody awful I have to really try and speak Irish, but I think I'm improving, that wasn't hard of course.

Do you remember that little nut I was telling you

about? I think he'll have me in a nut house before I go home, he takes fits and when I don't speak to him he won't eat his food. He's made a right daddy out of me. Do you know who was down here yesterday? McGuirk and County, they were starving so one of the lads went in to one of the shops and knocked off a big bunch of bananas. Davitt got an apple tart for them. They tried to get into the *céilí* last night but they were thrown out on account of their long hair. They left this morning but at dinner hour who do we meet, but Brían Byrne, Paul and Dick Rodgers we'll soon have the whole of Rialto down. Speaking of *céilís*, I love (you) the way you told me about the great time ye had at the 5 and asked what were the *céilís* like. Well they are crap with a big C, all you hear is an old idiot up on the stage giving out most of the time. He put me up on the stage the other night for being over the girls side (girls side at a dance, did you ever hear the like) when I asked him what was I up for, he nearly hit me. Did you got to Stella's house last Sunday? I hear you got a job, congrats, but don't work too hard.

If (God forbid) you are going to Belfast at the end of August, when will you be back? I suppose Mary told you that George and I were thinking of phoning ye some day next week. Mary said Monday or Tuesday I think we'll make it Monday, about 8 o'clock if that's all right with ye.

Well I think thats about all I have to say for now. Please write soon, looking forward to speaking to you on Monday.
All my love
Anthony
PS I really miss you down here.

From:	Patricia Byrne
Age:	16
Year:	1967
Home:	Dublin
Gaeltacht:	Arranmore, County Donegal

Colaiste Cróna
Arranmore
County Donegal
4 August 1967

Dear Mary

Hope that everything went as you wished on Monday and that you have stopped crying. I'm dying to know about Wednesday night, Gerald, Monday night Peter Mooney, India Tea Centre, the new house – in fact everything as this place is dead and we are just living on memories. (even me). All we hope is that you haven't written to Peadair. There are at the most five eligibles, three of which you would look at and only one is fabulous but is too young. (Don't breathe a word to anybody about it.)

Well I suppose I should start at the beginning. When we got to Navan Road we discovered we had many rivals. The journey was very tiring and we reached Burtonport at 6.00 that evening. We got the third boat accross and as we got near the boat laden with bags this boy about seventeen or eighteen took my cases, proud me. I fell in love immediately. The next morning Mary discovered his name is Pearse. He has a friend that we nickname 'Denim' as he dresses nice. Another friend we call 'Aran' who is quite good-looking and is from Cavan. They are the only eligibles and they are staying near us.

Yesterday afternoon at dancing lessons they were sitting opposite us. They went out to 'the juke box' and when they came back they sat beside us and seemed friendly. 'Denim' smiled a few times. Our classes were fixed out and they were put in our class.

Last night we started to get ready for the *céilí* at about 6.30. Alice and I washed our hair and Alice plugged in the iron. Bídí was sitting looking and suddenly Allie let the iron fall. When she picked it the handle was in two. You can imagine Mary and I! I had to go into the bedroom for fear Bídí would see me laughing. Bídí kept saying 'Íosa Críost the iron is broken' etc.

Well we went to the *céilí*. Mary was a real hit with the little kids. A '*rogha na mná*' was announced and just then Pearse walked in. You know me! I asked him up. He's real nice and lives in Drimnagh.

After the dance he left the hall. I was kicking myself. None of his friends were in either. At about twenty to ten he came in and a dance was announced and he asked me up . . . the *ceilí* ended at 10.00.

We were having our supper and Peadair came in with one of the other teachers. He was holding an enormous torch and informed us that there were 'blackguards' of Scottish campers who would most likely knock at the windows during the night and that we were to avail of the torch. The house is only a cottage and our bed is beside the window. We were listening to *Pop Call* and Alice was writing to Paul. When she put out the light, I remembered no more.

The next morning we were informed that the boys had been knocking at the window. Mary heard them but neither I nor Alice did. Bídí ran out after them and she said that there were the students from Duffys and that's where Pearse etc. are staying. So here's hoping.

I am writing at the moment in bed and Alice is reading *Macbeth*. We are hoping for good things tonight. This morning Pearse and 'Denim' and another fella were sitting behind us in school. After dinner 'Aran' said 'hello' to us. Last night at the *ceilí* they sat beside us for a while. And 'Denim' and Pearse were friendly.

The weather is terrible. We didn't go out tonight. After dinner an islander asked us to a dance which would last from 2.00 am to 6.00 am. The island is really beautiful and the beaches are gorgeous. One of them is like the beach in Portrane.

Our house is very far away from the hall and the school. The food wasn't so bad to-day but we have bread morning, noon and night. Well I hope you aren't getting too many scalds in the India Tea Centre. Tell them all I was asking for them, especially Bridget. Mary, please write soon and tell us all the news.

Lots of kisses

Patricia xxxxxxxxxxxx

c/o Coláiste Cróna
Arranmore
County Donegal
Thursday 6.55 pm [August 1967]

Dear Mary

Glad to receive your letter and hear all the good news. There was plenty of 'I love you' on Monday night Mary (lucky her). Her letter was also rosmantic. Well, Mary, I hope you are enjoying life because we are.

If you recall mention of a young teacher (Joe) last week, anyway, a mighty big crush has hit me. He teaches us in school and he is just gorgeous, really fab! On Monday night, being a bank holiday there was a '*ceilí mór*' and because it was over at 12.15, a teacher escorted us home – none other than Joe. Previously the islanders (dossers) had been pestering us at night knocking at the windows. Joe started talking to us about the islanders and asked us to show him them. We were walking along the road and suddenly we met the dosser. Joe started shining the torch on your man and put his arm around me – Patricia was in her 'seventh heaven' and has been ever since. On Tuesday night we went on a '*súilóid*'. He was with us all the time but naturally 'nothing comes from nothing' and as per usual being born under a lucky star??? (I don't think) I just am alone. Don't say anything to the boys about him though.

Well enough about lovely Joe. It is now 11.20 pm and we have just returned from another '*suilóid*'. As usual, Mary, being steeped in luck is almost certain to hit it off with a student teacher. He's good looking but is a bit sloopy and

50

dresses awful. Best of a bad bunch is what I say! He wasn't on the *súilóid* tonight however but here's hoping. As for Alice she received a letter from the 'mod lad' yesterday. Imagine her face! She's after a fab fellow (Louis Armstrong) and the Liz O'Shaugh is rubbing off on her for '*rogha na mban*' at the céilí. I nearly exploded when he sat near us in school and waited for us going home. That was this morning. Things were looking bright but alas! disillusion-ment! he asked Mary up at the *céilí*. (She's looking at me now, lying down in her dolly pyjamas). He never (Allie told me to add in his name is Fat Slob Lowery. Do you remember the story of 'Lowery, the King with horse's ears') uttered a word to her on the *súilóid*.

Well as for me, on Tuesday afternoon Mary and I were on the tennis courts playing when Seán comes along his girl and Rory, a friend of his. Seán and Mimi then started playing tennis and we were talking to Rory. Very goofey but is starting university. We left and I lend Rory my racket. That evening on the *súilóid* we were with Joe (that's another story) but Rory and Tom (Mary's lad) were trying to talk to us but I had no time being with Joe. At the end of our hill I asked Rory had he got my racket. His face coloured and he said 'Is it alright if we return it tonight at about 2.00 am.' We thought the holiday was beginning but they stood us up! Now we don't know what the situation is.

We all have been dying sick. Mary got a parcel full of goodies today. How did the boys get on in their Leaving, especially Peter! We went on a trip to Bloody Foreland last Saturday and we hope to be climbing Errigal to-morrow. Sorry to hear about the fingers been disjointed. I'm sure

I've been talking in riddles but I'm constantly been interrupted. Excuse the mistakes etc. Alice and Mary send their regards. Write a long letter soon.

Lots of love and kisses

Patricia and Mary

PS Are you coming up to see us? We want all news any little bit is valuable. Don't forget. Sorry for the writing being bumpy but I am lying crooked in bed. Till I hear the news. *Slán agus Dia duit.*

c/o Coláiste Cróna

Arranmore

County Donegal

August 1967

Dear Mary

At the moment we are sitting in school, the three of us like sardines in the one seat. Glad to have received your letter on Saturday.

Much has happened since our last letter, some of it for the better and most of it for the worst! Alice is busy with a lad from Mayo. Mary is just about to claim a grinning witch sitting across from us at the moment, who robbed the student teacher. As for Patricia, she is having her second romance, ugh! He is from Dublin and even goes as far as calling up for me. On Sunday afternoon, while he was sitting in the kitchen, I climbed out the bedroom window and ran for all I was worth. I'm doing my utmost best to brush him off and I think he's getting the message. A Scottish boy has my address. Our romances are too involved to be put

on paper (our heads will be spinning with lies) so goodbye
till Friday.
Love and kisses
Patricia, Mary and Alice

From: *Lorna Siggins*
Age: *14*
Year: *1974*
Home: *Sligo*
Gaeltacht: *Gortahork, County Donegal*

c/o Coláiste Uladh
Gort a Choirce
County Dún na nGall
11 July 1974

Dear Mum and Dad

I hope you are all well. I am as well as can be after a
lot of *walking*. We have to walk everywhere from our house
to the *colaiste*, twice a day. The classes are on in the
mornings and the *ceilí* is at night. We will be going for a
swim on the beach later this week, and we will probably
have to walk there too.

The brown bread is very good but some of the other
grub is not. Our *bean an tí* doesn't smile very much, and
maybe it is because she has noticed that we don't like the
puddings. It is a funny jelly and custard mix and a few of
the others have flushed it down the toilet. The toilet is at
one end of the room and the kitchen is at the other.

The father [priest] is also very strict. He has black hair and his face goes quite red when he is talking. One fella from Terenure College has already got a warning about speaking in English and the next time he is caught he will be sent home.

The father follows us home from the *ceilí* at nights in his Volkswagen Beetle. I don't know how he could know what we are talking, but he got out a few times to give out to people. The *ceilí* is great but I don't know how we are going to remember all the steps. Swinging round is the best part but you have to watch you don't get hammered.

I am OK for money but I have spent a bit more than I thought. It would be great to get some letters, because some people get them every day.

Hope the boys and Anne and Spike are well,
Love Lorna

Colaiste Uladh
Gort a Choirce
County Dun na nGall
16 July1974

Dear All

Thanks a million for the postal order which has come in very handy. There is only one shop here but the chocolate seems to be more expensive than at home. I get a bit hungry because some of the food is a bit difficult to eat. We can't really help ourselves and I get a bit peckish at night.

The beach at Machaire Rabhartaigh is amazing. We went there last Saturday and it was a long walk, but it was warm when we got in. We might be going to Mount Errigal next weekend if the weather is right. Some of the *muinteoiri* came and also the father, in his Volkswagen. He has sent one of the boys home, and some of us who jumped into some rushes in a bog hole for a dare got a warning. I don't know what he was getting so worked up about because I am sure we weren't shouting in English when we got wet. Somebody else was singing 'Yellow Submarine' though.

I hope all is well at home and that someone is taking Spike for walks. There are a few dogs here but they look a bit scrawny. If you could send some more letters it would be great, because some people get post every day.

Lots of love

Lorna

From: *Orla Kennedy*
Age: *14*
Year: *1976*
Home: *Dublin*
Gaeltacht: *Spiddal, County Galway*

10 July 1976

Dear Catriona

I like Spiddal. It's not such a culchie place after all. I keep been called a 'Dublin Jackeen' here by Mick Murphy, a boy in my Irish class who's from County Kildare – tell you more about him later! Mary Pugh and Roisin O'Neill from our school are in my class here along with fifteen others. Boys and girls mix – great.

Learning Irish is not so bad. It's a lot more fun than school. We spend a good deal of time learning Irish songs. I'll teach you a few when I get home. There's about an hour of reading and grammer stuff, but it's OK.

Colaiste Connacht is up on a hill and is quite old. It looks out over Spiddal Bay. We go swimming there every day if the weather is good, which it's been so far and then get let into the town in the afternoon if we want. There's a chip shop if you're starving which comes in handy. Myself and Eithne go down to the rocks by the sea after supper, just across the road from the house. It's great to smell the sea air and you certainly don't get donkey's in the gardens around Knocklyon!

I'm staying in a house just down the road from the college. Most of the rest of the girls from our class are staying up over the hills on the other side of the village, so I get to stay out later cause I'm closer to home. We have to be back by 7 pm for supper. Our *Bán an Tí* makes us all kneel down and say the rosary in Irish before bed – holy God! Siobhan Meehan has Miss Ronan staying with her, poor sod. Guess what – Miss Ronan has false teeth. Well, according to Siobhan – but you never know with her.

There's a *ceili* every Friday night in the college which is gear. I go along to the hall with Eithne and Maeve from County Meath who share my room at our house. I like them, and we've become friends. Eithne has some brilliant make-up and we put on a little up before we go out. Mr Culliton is on the watchout all the time for messing and make-up and speaking in English and if your caught you get sent home.

Can you believe it, Imelda Smith was sent home for smoking a cigarette down at the beach and speaking English. Bet her Ma will be mad at her.

Anyway, the *ceili* is greak crack. Last Friday, I got asked out to dance by Mick Murphy four times. He walked me home after and kissed me. So I reckon I get to first base before you eh? Eithne says he's brilliant and good looking. Maybe so. Anyway, you might get to meet him. He's going to visit his aunt and uncle in Rathfarnham in August. *So we'll see!*

When are you going on your hols? My mum says we might get to see you cause we'll be going back to Mayo later in the summer for a few weeks. Maybe you can come and stay with us for a bit. I wish you had been allowed to go to the Gaeltacht with me. What do you think, next year?

Love

Orla

From: *Máire Colgan*
Age: *9*
Year: *1980*
Home: *Dublin*
Gaeltacht: *Ring, County Waterford*

Coláiste na Rinne
Dúngarabhán
Phortlairge
3 July 1980

Dear Mummy

It is still great fun down here. We get beef nearly every day for lunch. It is raining today and it is quite cold. In my last letter I forget to tell you that we start classes at 10 o'clock, then at eleven we have a ten-minute break, after that we work till 12 o'clock at 12 we have an hour break we come back at 1 and work till 2 and we have another ten-minute break then at 3 we have dinner and we are off for the day. I am in class 13. I also didn't tell you I am a sub on a basketball team. If we win, everyone on the team including the sub gets a medal. So pray that we win. Vanessa got her stitches out on Tuesday. I don't think there's anything else to say so

Goodbye and love always

Máire xoxox

PS I hope you got my last letter and I am sorry about this letter being so uninteresting.

Coláiste na Rinne
Dungarabhan
County Phortlairge
11 July 1980

Dear Mummy

It is still great fun down here. There is nothing exciting to say except we went for a swim and the water was freezing, we were only in for about ten minutes. I received your letter and was delighted to hear from you. (By the way this is my fourth letter). The basketball matches are going very well we are into the semi-finals, so you'd never

know and my team said that I am a player now because the other girl never turns up. We play squash now and then and it is good fun. I never told you in my last letters that I wrote to Nadine, Uncle Eoin and Auntie Joan, Uncle Fosco and Auntie Eilis. That's all I have to say for now so,
Love always
Máire xoxoxo
PS Please write and give my love to Hazel.

From: *Barra McCabe*
Age: *12*
Year: *1984*
Home: *Dublin*
Gaeltacht: *Barra spent a year in Ring College, County Waterford*

Scoil na Leanbh
An Rinn
Dúngarbhán
County Phortláirge
7ú Mean Fomhair 1984

Dear Mum and Dad
I hope you are well. I am having quite good fun. I get homesick a few times but I *always* get over that. Thank you very much for the laces the cartriges and the stamps. I miss you both very much Donogh and Caoimhe are missed by me too. We were talking in the dorm last night and Frank caught us we were all shivering like mad then in the

59

morning we had to pick up every piece of paper in a field and in the scrap yard and we had to do other things too. Dad I need a red biro and I need too more stamps please. I played on the big squash court Donogh it wrecks you. I played on the small ones too but they are not as much fun.

Mum your apple tart came in very handy. I have not drank your fizzy orange yet. I still have plenty of tuck left. I got the second letter today but I could not read some parts of it. Teacher told us to right this note.

Enclosed herewith find poliomyelitis form. The *bean an tí* has requested to have same returned not later than Friday next the 14th inst. as the doctor will be calling to the school that day. Dad could you get me a dictionary and an atlas please. We had fish and chips and beans for dinner today. Frank would not let us have tuck today so that is 85p down the drain to be collected at end of term. We were counting how many people in the dorm and we counted £20 to the school over that.

Slán for now.

Love from

Barra

Scoil na Leanbh
Coláiste na Rinne
Dúngarbhán
County Phortláirge
Dé hAoine 28ú Meán Fomhair 1984

Dear Mum and Dad

I hope you are well. Thanks very much for coming to visit

Patrick and me. We really enjoyed the day out and especially the dinner. We had sausages and chips today for dinner it was OK. Mum I am sorry but I forgot to tell you that Patrick and I need a nailbrush each. Dad I hope your back is fully better. Dad will you and Mum be giving us another visit before halloween. I played my squash match last Sunday, the Sunday I was with you and I lost eleven nil that is very bad. Donogh will tell you why it is so bad. Thanks for the letter but I have not yet had a chance to read it. I have really no news for you because everything is quiet here. But I will try to make the letter as interesting as I can.

Barry Collery fell of a wall. Somebody pushed him off it and he had to go to hospital but he was alright. I am getting my tuck shop food today and am looking forward to it very much. Thank you very much for all the tuck Mum and Dad. I am really enjoying it. This is what is gone already – the apple tart, the apple cake, and the eight little cakes. They were all lovely especially the apple tart. I am sorry the letter looks so rushed but I have to write a postcard to Auntie Barbera for giving us the lovely tuck. I have not yet got the postcard off to uncle Michael. The rosary beads are coming very handy Dad. They seem to make the rosary go much better. I will have to go now. I am sorry it is so short.

Slán agus beannacht.

Love from

Barra

Scoil na Leanbh
Coláiste na Rinne
Dúngarbhán
County Phortláirge

Dear Mum and Dad,
    I hope you are well. Could you please tell Grandpop happey birthday from me. I have nothing really to tell you this week, so I will make the letter quick and snappy because I don't want you to get board with all the gorey details. Caoimhe I hope the debs goes well and tell Jim I was sorry to hear about his pigtails and I hope he gets them back. Mum I wrote to granna so look in her place for letters. I hope the drinks party goes well with Mr and Mrs Manoge. Tell Ned I am going to write to him so he better be prepared because its going to be very hard to handle.
    Dad I hope your back get better soon.
    Slán agus beannacht.
Love from
Barra

Scoil Na Leanbh
Coláiste na Rinne
Dúngarbhán
County Phortláirge
Dé hAoine 9ú Samhain 84

Conas atá sibh a Mhamaí agus a Dhaidí.
    Tá mé ag scríobh as Gaeilge mar tá an múinteor ag déanamh iarracht hard ag cuardú le Gaeilge.

Seol síos mo Baptismal cart do mo chomhnearta go tapaidh. Más é do thoil é.

Conas atá an Rabbit agus an Gunea Pig agus an Avery Caoimhe agus Donagh.

Táim ag fáil an Gaeilge decair anois a Mhamaí.

Tá mé ag súil le cuairt.

Go raibh míle maith agaibh dos na laethanta saoire deasa.

A Dhaidí tá scéim marc dúbh sa rang seo anois.

Tá an Gaeilge ag teacht chugaim anois.

Shroicheamar ar áit seo ar leathuair tar éis a trí.

Cuir glaoch guthain orm.

Slán agus beannacht anois.

Love from

Barra

Scoil na Leanbh
Coláiste na Rinne
Dúngarbhán
County Phortláirge
16ú Samhain 1984

Conas atá sibh a Dhaidí agus a Mhamaí

Fuair mé do litir agus chonaic me an photograph, thosaigh me ag gáire faoi Caoimhe agus Padraig.

Fuair mé céad i mo stair test a Mhamaí ach níorbh teistenna na Nollaig iad.

Tá mé ag déanamh iarracht caint as Gaeilge.

Fuair an Rang ban from tuck mar bhí an Rang ag caint as Béarla.

Tá mé ag súil le cuairt.

Seol síos mo Baptisimal cart do mo chomneartha go tapaidh más é do thoil é.

How are you Mum and Dad

I hope you are great.

I got the letter and I saw the photographs.

I started to laugh when I saw Caoimhe and Patrick.

I got a hundred in my history test but it was not our Christmas test.

I am trying to speak Irish. The class got band from tuck because we were speaking English.

Please send down the Baptismal certs as quickly please.

Slán agus beannacht.

Love from Barra

Scoil na Leanbh
Coláiste na Rinne
An Rinn
Dúngarbhán
County Phortlárige
30ú Samhain1984

Conás atá sibh a Mhamaí agus a Dhaidí

Go raibh míle míle maith agaibh don chuairt. Fuair mé Kellogs Cornflakes van. Bhain mé taitneamh as an gcuairt. Seol síos cotaí dúbh más é do thoil é. Cónas ata an guinea pig agus an rabbit. Tá mé ag doing iascaireacht in Éire a Mhamaí.

Hi Mum and Dad

Thank you very much for the visit it was great fun. I got the Kellogs Cornflakes van. I really enjoyed the visit. Please send down a black suit coat as I am dressing up as a priest in the fancy party before we go home. How are the guinea pig and the rabbit. We are doing fishing in Ireland its great. *Slán agus beannacht.*

Love from

Barra

Scoil na Leanbh
Coláiste na Rinne
An Rinne
Dúngarbhán
County Phortláirge
12ú mí na Nollag 1984

Dear Caoimhe and Donogh

I hope you are both well.

Hopefully there will be a fancy dress party on Saturday for all the school in the hall.

There will be a *ceolchoirm* on Saturday morning or Monday morning in the school.

I am really looking forward to getting home and see you all.

I'm not sure how much the bill is for the train but Mum and Dad will know that.

I will have to say bye now so

Slán agus beannacht.

Scoil na Leanabh
Coláiste na Rinne
Dúngarbhán
County Phortláirge
3ú Bealtaine 85

A Chláinn Dhíl

Conas atá sibh?

Ní bheidh aon staidear amárach (Dé hAoine). Ní thuigim do litir a Mhaim mar sin níl fhios agam cad atá ar siúl abhaile. Tá tuc inniu agus tá mé ag súil le sin. Tá mo bhróga nua ana dheas orm agus tá mé ana shásta leo.

Tá rás 100 metres céad agus rás native agus chuaigh me isteach sa 100 metres agus tháinig mé deirneach.

Níl aon nuacht agam ach tá na pictuire ag teacht ón fear a thóg é.

Go raibh míle maith agaibh arís don deireadh seachtanna maith.

Slán agus beannacht.

Gra mór

ó

Barra

From: *Fíona Ní Chinnéide*

Age: *15*

Year: *1986*

Home: *Dublin*

Gaeltacht: *Coláiste Bhríde, Rannafast, County Donegal*

Coláiste Bhríde

Rannafast

Annagry

County Donegal

30 July 86

(Alternative address: 50 miles from everywhere, Back of Beyond!)

Hi parents + Níall! (at least – *Dia dhaoibh*)

I decided to write a letter, because well there's nothing else to do! Ah no, seriously, I just wrote to say I arrived safely. So (drum roll):

    'I arrived safely!'

The journey was long and boring! But once we got to about Omagh it seemed like no time before we reached Letterkenny. Hang on, I'm all confused now! What I meant was: the journey between Omagh and Letterkenny seemed short enough. When we came to the largest mountain (after Letterkenny) I thought to myself 'is that Erigall' thinking it was the largest mountain but as we drove on another two large mountains came into view. A girl behind me started singing 'Erigall, Erigall' but still I was confused as to which one it was. At last, as we rounded the farthest one the

67

same girl cried 'Is that Erigall?' to which someone replied 'That's Erigall!'!

Well anyway, the house is nice. It's warm: except at night. We have one thin blanket each. I'm in a room of six (there are two others, one for four and one for two and I'm sharing a bunk with Tanya. The other four are: Deirdre, Fiona, Ciara and Ruth. Ruth is fourteen and the other two are fifteen, although you'd swear they were older.

The food is awful! Well, it's not that bad. For tea (when we arrived) we had cold beans on unbuttered toast, for breakfast we had toast (cold) with margarine (we reckon Stork) and for our latest meal burgers and potatoes and peas, soup, (I mean soup to start) and a pukey dessert of unflavoured whipped jelly, at least that's what we think it was? Barbara (thirteen) reckons it was saliva dyed pink!!! (pleasant).

Well, we heard the munchies [local teenagers] last night and I was *petrified*! I'm OK now. They were screaming and shouting and flashing lights!

Well, I'd better finish up

Slán

Fiona

PS I'm in class 4C

PPS I've demolished four packets of Polo already!

14 August1986

Dear Parents

I hope you got home safely, I did! I was sad until I reached the house, after a short outburst (boo!hoo!) I was OK. The *ceolchoirm* was terrific, Deirdre played brilliantly (on the clarinet). Her parents stayed to watch. The fella I was talking about, the anarchist vegetarian Conor who sang last time, sang again. It was gift doss. [an elevating experience]

There was a *céilí mór* last night with a fancy dress. OK parents you may disown me if you like (if you are of a nervous disposition skip next paragraph) but I went as a tart, yes a tart! Deirdre and Tanya did the same. I was 'Jonston' Deirdre was 'Mooney' and Tanya 'O'Brien'! Our slogan was – 'The freshest tarts going!' We had great fun. I wore fishnet tights, a plastic bag mini, studded belt and ordinary belt, black top, chains, lace and sizzling hot red lipstick!

As we neared the college we had a few second thoughts but it was too late to turn back, and as we walked across the yard a load of cheers and wolf-whistles were to be heard! Some of the costumes were hilarious. There was a pregnant nun, a pope, a-team, Pinochio, Greek gods – you name it. The crack was mighty – we even managed to get boys to walk us home (a third joined us). One of them was dressed as a judo player (to protect us). The food is the same as always. We are still basking in the memory of coleslaw, chicken and chips followed by ... *stop, stop, I can't stand it*! My mouth is foaming, slurp, slurp.

Well, I must admit, I'm dying to go home, although I know I'll cry on the last day. Talking about last days, time is flying. It's unbelievable. We only have five school days left (tomorrow Friday, is a day off)! Oh yeah, today's Níall's birfday. I wrote him a letter forgetting to say happy birfday so I sent a postcard as well. Don't write another letter here because I'll probably be home! The bus leaves here at 9.00 am with a seven-hour journey. I should arrive in Dublin at about 4.00 pm.

Well I'd better finish up. Love to you both.

Fíona

From:	*Conor McManamly*
Age:	*13/14*
Year:	*1986/1987*
Home:	*Dublin*
Gaeltacht:	*Camus, County Galway*

Coláiste Chamaus
23 July 86

Dear Mum and Dad

I'm lying in bed and its 8.35 pm. If you're wondering why I'm lying in bed its because I've just come home from the doctor's. I had a terrible pain last night and I got it again around an hour ago. The pain is like the one I had a few months ago and Seamus said it was a pulled muscle. The doctor (who was seven miles away, in Spideal) didn't say what it was, all he did was give me four tablets and said it will be OK. The house I'm staying is tiny. It's two miles from the college which takes around half an hour to walk five times a day. I have the worst *cinnere tí* (the person who looks after you and takes your complaints). He's fifteen. To make things worse I'm sleeping in the same room as him. The other person in my room is called

Eamonn. He is a Murphy! Job, a complete loner. In the next room is Fergal a ten year old who talks to himself and plays with the baby in the house. Next is Brian another loner. Then Shane he's a complete weirdo and then there's Rory (not Murphy) another loner. So as you can see I cannot stand staying in this house the only normal person around is the *bean an tí*. The college is tiny around the size of three prefabs. It's real boring all we do is play basketball and sing songs. All I want to do now is *go home* and don't say you'll get used to it after the first week there is no way I will. It's the complet opposite to what Kathleen Dillon said a great atmosphere (Ha!) Its great for the big fellos like John Dillon. All the big fellos see to be having a ball. Ali said he'd love to go home as well. I really miss both of you and I mean really miss. *Please*!! *Please*!! *Please*!! do something quick. I would love to be at home now. Will you write a letter and come up to collect me. You have to do something all around me is barron (and the village Spiddal is *seven* miles away) I cannot stand it any longer. Please *take me home!* The pain.

Please, please, please! Write back *immediately*. I can't wait to go.

Bye From Conor

PS I love you!

I love you too!

Tulach
Monday 28 July

Dear Mum and Dad and Elaine

2.10 pm. Things have completely changed. Like you said they would in the letter. When I was writing the letter I really badly wanted to go home mainly because of the pain it was really killing me. But when I went to the doctor the tablets he gave helped and I don't have it any more. There was a bug going around. That night I wrote the letter I got sick twice but I was OK in the morning. And the night after everyone in my house got sick except Stiofan my *cinnere tí* and me. In every other house at least one person got sick. Every one in my house is OK when I got to know them. My best friend in our house is Rory. He goes to Castleknock College. I have so much to tell you I don't know I'm going to remember it all! The day starts off with us getting up at 8.00 am and we get dressed and have our breakfast then take it in turns to wash and brush our teeth, etc. We leave our house at 9.15 am to get there at 10.00 am. Its three miles to the school. But when the sun is shining, I don't really mind the walk. When we arrive at the school we hang around a bit and then we go into the hall and sing '*Madin ag gealadh*'. Its sort of like the college 'Morning' National Athem then we go to our classes. The classes are great fun. Its really amazing how much Irish you learn in one class. We have three classes with a break in between each one. We have a different teacher for each class theres around 8 teachers all together and I like them all. One lives in laurel lodge. (I have to go to the college now as soon as

72

I come back I'll continue the letter).

9.30 pm. I've just got in, the *fear an tí* gave us a lift. We met him on the road with 2 miles to go. It was a bumpy ride because as soon as one wheel comes out of a pothole another one goes in.

I had to wear my full rain gear because it was lashing rain today. Its terrible having to walk three miles to the college. In one day we walk twelve miles and that is the only thing I dislike about the Irish college. All the girls houses are in a big bunch across the road from the college.

I have met loads of new friends. I nearly know the name of everyone here, well quite a lot of people. We're going to Galway on Friday or Wednesday. We have a *céilí* every night there good fun. I learnt around four dances so far.

I don't mind if you don't come up it's up to you. But if you do there's a couple of things I'd like you to bring, my blue jacket, my navy jumper with the grey line on the v-neck. My Levis jumper the thick one. A pack of cards if you can find a pack in the house. One pack of odour eaters. The ones I have are size six and my Puma runners are size five. I'm wearing my new Nike runners all the time because when I wear the Puma ones (A) They get terribly smelly and when we're in the room the smell of socks is terrible, (B) They make my socks smelly. But when I wear my Nike runners there's no smell. And I can wear the same pair of socks for *at least* three days without them getting a bit smelly, odour-eaters are brilliant.

I suppose you didn't by the Sin 1. That would be a great surprise when I come home. (Hint, Hint!)

I have loads more to tell you but I wouldn't be able to fit it all into the envelope so I'll tell you when you come up to visit me or when you come up to collect me for Cork. If we go. Thanks for the last letter. You don't know how great it is to hear from you.

Bye for now.

Conor

I love you!!!

I love you.

Tuesday morning 29 July

8.45 am

I just finished my breakfast and I was thinking I would like you to come up maybe you could come up at the weekend. Write and tell me what your doing. I am going to wash me teeth now. I'll post this letter today.

Bye for now.

Love

Conor

I love you!!

Colaiste Chamuis

An Tulach

Baile na h-Abhann

County na Gaillimhe

Wednesday 30 July

3.00 pm

Dear Mum and Dad and Elaine,

I received your second letter this morning. I posted my

second letter yesterday. You've probably got it by now. I also posted a post card to Nana, and Paul and Sive. I asked Paul and Sive to phone you to tell you to send Grannies address and a few 28p stamps with your next letter.

Cardinal O'Fea (I'm not sure if thats the right spelling) visited the college today all he did was, stay a few minutes listening to some songs. He also sang one song himself. We don't have to go back to the college until 7.00p.m. because Cardinal O'Fea (*arís*) was saying Mass and the 9 classes singing at it.

Theres a new rule here that if one word of English is spoken your on the dishes for a day. We're all so used to putting in words of English here and there the original plan for the people on the dishes is totally wrecked. I'm on the dishes three days in a row with one other person each day. Its nothing serious though.

Colaiste Chamuis came yesterday. We had a big *ceilí* between both colleges. There was so many we had to have it out in the yard. At the end the teachers sang a song and a few acted it out. For example, the song was 'Rose of Tralee', one person hold up a Rose and another a map of Ireland with a big circle around Tralee. It was all in Irish of course. Stiofán (my *cinnere tí*) has just come in and told me if I wash the lunch boxes and the flasks now I'll get off one day on the dishes. That's great!

We were going to go swimming today but it was to cold. We're going on a *toras* (*arís*) on Friday (whatever that is!) I think its going around Galway and stopping every now and again. We'll also be going to the caves in Clare and maybe Lesiureland.

In our house four peoples parents have come up so maybe you will come up on Saturday or Sunday as I suggested in the last letter.

I can't wait to go to Cork. But remember we'll have to be back to collect my books on 27 August. I can't think of much else to write.

Bye for now.

Love Conor

I love you!

PS Write back immediately.

Colaiste Tulach
5 August 1986 1.00 pm

Dear Mum, Dad and Elaine

Thanks very much for coming up to see me. I enjoyed that day. I received a letter from Mimi this morning she sent five pounds in it.

I didn't got to school today because last night I woke up at four o'clock and got sick and around two minutes after that Eamonn got sick. Eamonn was nearly going home yesterday because on our way to the college he read out a note on the shop window in English. Then when we got to the college Steafon told big Steafon that Eamonn read out note. Eamonn was sent back to the house and packed his bags. While he was packing his bags big Steafon rang up his mum and his mum told Steafon that Eamonn's sister died three months ago from lucimia and because of that Steafon didn't send Eamonn home.

Did you receive my other letter with the drawings of

Steafon and my friends. I haven't received Paul's letter yet and I'm posting Grannie's and Auntie Mel's post cards today.

I feel a little bit better now and I think I'll go back to the colaiste after we've had our dinner. I'm looking forward to going to Cork.

Bye for now.

Love Conor

PS Write back immediately.

4.30 pm

I'm writing this because there is absolutely nothing to do. Steafoan won't let us go to the shop. He's the worst *cinnere tí* in Tulach. Every other house is allowed go to the shop. It closes at six and we don't leave until 6.15 pm to go back to the college. He's only fifteen. And he ruins the whole three weeks.

The food is very nice in my house. I would say I have the best house foodwise. If you heard the descriptons of other houses food you would faint.

In the last letter you said walking will keep me trim. You're right. If you saw the roads that we walk on!

I don't know why they don't build a straight road.

I better go now.

Love

Conor

I love you!

Colaiste Camus
Tualach
23 July 1987

Good News!!
Hi Mum . . . Hi Dad . . . Hi Elaine

First of all I'm having a great time, now you can stop worrying. I'm in a brilliant house with thirteen in it. My *cinnerie tí* is dead on he is a messer, his name is Dathai (David). Theres four people in my room Dathaí, Stiofan (not last year's *cinnere tí* . . . Thank God), Proncias and me. Everyone in my house is dead on, except one fellow, he's around 11. We stopped in Moate yesterday. There was nothing to do, but we only stayed for half an hour. We went through Athlone and half an hour later we realised we had to pick people up. So we went all the way back to pick them up.

Rory's in the house I was in last year. Theyv'e got an extension so now instead of seven people there's twelve. Most of the people I knew well are back.

This morning we went to the college to be put in classes . . . There's six classes A, B, C, D, E, F. A is for people who have done their leaving, B is for those who going to do it next year, C is for those who have just finished their inter, that's the class I'm in. I'll tell you why in a minute, D is for those who are doing it next year, thats the class I should be in, and E and F is for those who are in 1st year or under. I'm not in the D class because it was to big . . . so they moved the people out of it who were in Tualach last year so I was moved. I prefer that because I know more people in C.

Excuse my writing, but I'm writing it in class, because at the moment they're writing out and learning the '*Amhran an Colaiste*', which I already know.

That's all I really have to say.

Oh yeh! Theres a load of new teachers some are terrible some are nice.

Bye for now.

I miss you (but not near as much as last year which is meant to be good)

I love you.

Conor

Colaiste Camus

29 July 1987

Hi Mum, Dad and Elaine

I'm having a brilliant time here. It's Wednesday and I'm still waiting for a letter. Please get everyone to send a letter its terrible when their giving out the letters and there's none for you.

As I said in the last letter I'm on the bus which is brilliant. The food is OK but not as good as last year. The milk is a bit weird, we've come to the conclusion that it comes straight out of a cow. There's two cows outside the kitchen window. The *bean an tí* tells the *fear an tí* to get some milk, he goes out with a bucket comes in with a full bucket of *milk*!

At the moment I'm sitting in my room on my bed (the bottom bunk) . . . (of a bunk bed) and Stiofan and Cathal are having a game of Spit (a card game). Dathí (*cinnere tí*) is telling everyone who wants to get money out of the post office is to take their post office book with them and Proncais is cursing his head off because everyone is using his deodrant. Brian is having a deodrant fight with Liam. Its probably Proncaise's deodrant and I'm writing this letter to you its 2.20 pm and we'll be getting the bus at 3.00 pm. Oh . . . Cathal just won the card game . . . anyway when we get to the college we'll either play sport or go to our groups. Groups is when three or four houses join together to do drama and near the end they put the play on, on stage. Our group is going to do a play during 1916 with P. Pearse etc. in it we sing songs, read poetry and act.

The weather up here is pretty good. Excuse my writing but I'm writing on my bed with everyone fighting and crying and screaming and singing in front of me . . . 'Proncais got his deodrant back!' . . . We went to the beach the other day it was pretty good. There was loads of fishes in the water and one fellow took one out, thinking it was dead . . . but . . . it wasn't he threw it at the girls and it started moving the whole beach started laughing. Rory Murphy ran to the rescue and threw the fish back in.

The classes are great crack. The three biggest messers in the college are in my class. Our house won the question time. We'll get our prizes on prizegiving night (the last night). I'm looking forward to getting your letter. I better go now because I'm about to have a game of cards.
Slán. I love you.
Conor
PS *Gur bhfuil tú ag iarriad (not spelt right) a fhios níl mé ag dul amach le aon caílin fós.*

Colaiste Camus
Tuesday 3 August 1987

Dia dhuit

Dear Mum, Dad and Elaine

Where are the letters, a week and a half has gone by its Tuesday, the letters have been given out and I only received 1 letter from you which was a few days ago and one from Mimi. I *hope* I'll have one tomorrow!!

Anyway apart from receiving one letter in a week and a half I'm having a great time. Our house won the song competition, it turned out brilliant. It's going to be one of the college songs. Everyone is singing it now.

On Sunday morning we went for a walk across the bog it was brilliant we were running through real Galway bogs across stone walls, getting chased by bulls and at some stage we reached a lake it was amazing it was like the valley of the diamonds with a big lake at the bottom. You'd love it Mum. Theres loads of heather.

Proncais who was in my room is moving to another house and Brendan is moving in. He's moving in because a few months ago he broke his leg and it gets sore if he walks on it too much, so he's moving to our house, which is on the bus.

I'm looking forward to seeing you at the weekend. There will be a note on the door of the college hall or school, check both doors. It will tell you where the teacher's house is (take note of the cross roads and it will be easy to find). Go to the teacher's house and they'll tell you how to get to my house. If you come at the time I told you in the last letter, you won't have to go to all the bother of finding my house. Oh! when your coming up will you bring one, two or three or four or five or six packets of fun size bars. Seriously bring one or two packets preferably Mars or Marthon.

Today we're going to Carraroe to play a football match against Coláiste Coloumba (another college). It will be good crack. On Friday we went to Coláiste Camus after the tour we had a big *ceilí* I met loads of people from my class and from 6th class. It was great.

I'm really looking forward to seeing you.

Slán . . . *keep writing* or start writing.

I love you.

Conor

From: *Renate Ní Uigin*
Age: *15–17*
Year: *1987–89*
Home: *Dublin*
Gaeltacht: *Camus, County Galway*

Colaiste Chamuis
Camus
County na Gaillimhe
22 July 1987

Dear Mum, Dad, Keith and Michelle
Hi all

I got here grand and safe. I'm a *cinnire tí* as you know.

There are eight other girls here, four disincluding me have been here before but I only know one of them.

In our letters we have to adress them in Irish and as I don't know any adress except mine in Irish I cheated and put Granny's and Nanas adresses in English and gave them to Laura to post as she passes the post box which is very handy. Later:

We were playing basketball this afternoon – we have to choose between basketball and volleyball. I took basketball. Although our team lost 8-6 I actually scored two baskets. I have never before gotten *one* basket and then two in one game! We also have to play soccer we were playing that yesterday our team lost 2-0. We were at Mass this evening so we'll have a free morning tomorrow in which we're meant to tidy our rooms and wash our clothes but *bean an tí* is going to wash them in the washing machine (Hooray). So that's that. However, there will be a song competition between the different houses on Wednesday and the house has to write a song so we'll be doing that in the morning.

I don't think I've any more news.

Write soon.

Slán.

Grá do gach duine

Renate xxxxxxxx

23 July 87

Hi its me again. Its now Thursday and as our letters haven't been posted yet I decided to write a bit more.

We're just after having dinner – chicken carrots and potatoes with veg. Soup to start and cake to finish. It was only gorgeous. For breakfast we have orange juice cornflakes and tea and toast. All this morning was very boring. We were told to wait for the bus – it was coming at 9 am. It arrived at half past nine. When we got to the school we had to wait for another three-quarters of an hour for the teachers (typical). Then we were just sitting around talking and being talked to. We learnt Amhrán an Cholaiste then which was even more enthralling and then we went home.

It's quite good this house and the people in it.

Bye.

Love to all

Renate xxxxxxxx

Camus

24 July 1987 Friday

Hi All

The weather here is lovely and sunny but at times it can be a bit cold. I'm getting on grand at being a *cinnire* and the people in the house are really very nice. There were classes this morning. They divide the classes up by age and what year in school you're in. Last year I was in rang C but this year I'm in rang A – a big jump. We had fish for dinner today smoked cod and tinned peas yeuch. The cod wasn't that bad but I much prefer ray. I'm also writing to Granny and auntie today and Mary and George tomorrow. I'm sending Nana a card for her birthday. She won't get it in time but its the thought that counts.

I'll finish this letter tomorrow.

Bye

love Renate

Hi again

Its Saturday afternoon. Just finished my dinner of ham, turnip and tinned peas – dreadful. We get soup here instead of dessert. For dessert we get biscuits – how exciting. Yesterday the weather was lovely and I got sun on my face. I know because my nose was burning up – more freckles. However today was not as nice it is quite cold. We practiced for Mass this morning, very boring, just saying mass and singing hymns.

Camus

29 July 87

Hi all

(Sorry about the red pen but at the moment I can't find my blue one). How are you all, I'm very put out because this is my third letter and I haven't received one from you yet. I presume you have written. I have also written to Granny and Aunty and Mary and George and not received a reply. I haven't received the post for today so I'm hoping I'll get a letter.

[Later]

I'm back, it's evening now and I didn't receive a letter

so I'm very angry. Are you coming down at all? Please *write* soon and let me know, because if and only if you are or when Pat is, give her my black jacket. It's getting pretty cold down here especially in the evenings. And also a bag of mini Crunchies or Mars or something like that they are very handy. The house is still good the dinner today wasn't brilliant:

Stew and jelly and cold lumpy custard for desert – no-one ate it and except for me and one other girl no-one ate the stew (aren't I very good). We had gigot chops yesterday and mince casserole on Mon. Hopefully tomorrow's dinner will be better. One girl in my house had to go home on Sunday to work in her father's office because the staff were sick, so there are only eight left in the house. Renate

Colaiste Chamuis
Camus
County na Gaillimhe
[July 1988]

Hi all

It's about ten to nine and we've arrived safely – though it took us long enough. We – our bus – arrived at Camus at half past four and had to wait for an hour and a half for the other buses to come and of course it was raining. We got to the house about seven and had tea etc.

The people in the house so far seem really nice – though guess what I got once again – the weirdo that was in my house last year. God help me. Catherine Somers is in my house and the *cinnirí* are OK – so its not too bad.

Keith got the best fellas house, he has two *cinnirí* one of whom is Douglas and Risteard the PC as well – he won't be talking in English I can tell you.

The bus – after everyone complaining re: parents – was emptied of cases etc so it was only two to a seat – pretty comfortable. I haven't got the room with a slumber-down this year but its just as good. Its great having been here before. The *bean* and *fear an tí* both knew me and so did all the children. Its really good.

I know this isn't long but it'll suffice. I only saw ye this morning.

See youse – don't worry about the grammar or spelling
Love
Renate

Camus
21 July 1989

Hi

I'm totally wrecked – we only reached the house at half past eight. We actually reached the school at 4.15 but one bus broke down between Ouchtar Ard (lovely spelling!) and Maam Cross – we took the back road as it ran out of diesel – they got some more but there wasn't enough so they had to go back for more! Well by the time they got to the school it was 7.20 – they had to wait for three hours on the bus and were raging.

The only rain we saw was in Dublin this morning by the way we left at ten to eleven but got down fairly quickly.

Though all today seemed a series of mishaps we couldn't leave the school till the other bus came then when we reached here all the cases were collected except one house's which I still don't know what happened to them. One boy then sent his case to one of the girls houses, another boy didn't know where he was meant to be and still doesn't for all I know – I'll have to wait till Aine (that wonderful woman) comes later.

I forgot my alarm clock when you're coming will you bring it down please.

The room I'm in has a window facing out front which means you can see the teachers' lights coming – very handy.

Keith has no voice left he's been singing so much he hasn't been singing outside like in front of the colaiste but everyone has heard him because himself and others Conor amongst them are singing/playing the guitar non stop in one of the class rooms.

I have to go now as its time to leave and *walk* and wait one hour for everyone to come (yet again).

See you next Saturday.

Bye

Lots of love

Renate

PS Áine came last night and we hadn't got the right list earlier so there was a big swop of rooms more chaos.

Well that's about all. I'll write again soon.

Love

Renate

From: *Keith Higgins*
Age: *13/14*
Year: *1987/1988*
Home: *Dublin*
Gaeltacht: *Camus, County Galway*

Dear Mam, Dad and Michelle

I am here all in one piece and I'm now sitting on the floor in my room writting this letter. I got one of the best houses in the whole place. We had a salad for tea which was very nice and so far the house has lived very much up to its name. There are three bedrooms in the house with two sets of bunk beds in each room. So that means twlve people in the house, the *b-an-tí* and *f-an-tí* are very nice and on the way to the house the man of the house came and took are bags and brought them all up to the house (in the car) and when we all arrived they were all layed out on the drive for us to take.

The bus journey was very long and trying but it was worth it all in the end. One bus got to the college first so we then had to wait for a half an hour for the Galway bus to come and then another half hour for the Bogger Bus and the second bus from our area to come.

C got here grand and he also got a good house.

I've made a good few friends all ready and all the blokes in my room are all very friendly and good to talk to.

So that's about it.

Bye

Keith

Monday 5 July [1988]

Hello family

At long last I might here you say. Well I decided on the very first day I would leave it till today and write an enormously long entertaining letter.

How are you all any way. Did you have a good time in Waterford.

I got your first letter about fruit-picking with Mary and Max, tremendously stimulating I must say. Mother, weren't you so lucky to find that fiver, God was really with you.

Dad thanks for the money and the note greatly appreciated and Mam for the biscuits etc very kind of you.

Just as well I didn't write sooner, I here there was or is?? a postal strike. Any way I myself am fine actually great, not looking forward to coming home. (Please take no offence).

Well to start off with my gaff is quite good, the food is good, not brilliant but good, there is only seven others in my house and I have only a three-mins walk to the 'cross bothar'.

There has been no trouble in my house, they all are all right. I have one total, total, total bogger, the worst, he sleeps with his grandmother, in the same bed, he doesn't go to school during the winter for he has to work on 'the farm', I could go on and on, but he is all right.

Any way, Murf is in Tí Sheáin Neil, my house last year. Elaine is in Tí Shéams Mhairtín Jane, Renate's house for three years so she is living in the lap of luxury. Her house (the people) are not the best, young etc. The blokes in my house are eleven yrs, and the rest are all 14.

We have to wash our clothes so that a bit of a bind but it all right the problem is getting them bloody well dry.

As for the weather it not too bad. We have had a good few nice days most just dry days which is good. But we also have had a few days with non stop rain. But then we go to the hall.

As for the hall, its nice but we spend too much time there the school is much better for some reason.

And now, that is every day nearly. We would walk from the school to the footie pitch just to have our tea. Because the teachers office is now in the hall in a room and all their stuff is there for their lunch etc. So 243 students have to change places for to eat a few sandwiches just so the teachers can have there tea in the hall.

Most days we would play basketball or volley ball or else football.

On Wednesday last we went on our tour. It was totally poxy. Listen to this, we went first to the village where the film *The Field* was made, stayed there for fifteen minutes then went all the way to Westport I think, well Sligo somewhere to a beach, stayed on the beach for three hours then spent another two hours in the buses eventually got to Spidal. Bleedin Spidal, stayed there for ten to fifteen mins and went home.

I was unable to buy anything because there is nothing in Spidal and absolutely nothing in the 'Field' village.

Last night, that is Sunday night, oh Jesus no, Saturday night, Sorry my bearings have totally gone as to what day it is, the song competition was on. My house came second to a hopeless song from Tí Tess (girls house). My song anyway was well responded to. It was 'Day in the Life', a Beatles tune. I played the guitar. And you see, the words were totally different than anyone elses. They were about the sourondings etc. (my thoughts), very serious.

And Aíne and P, totally love it. They called it a 'classic' so I was well pleased.

So that's it, I hope you enjoyed your long entertaining read about Camus.

Say hello to everyone for me.

I look forward to seeing you.

Lots of love

Keith

PS This is the tenth page. Didn't I do well.

PPS I hope you can understand everything, it's quite difficult writing quickly in English again.

Slán

Le grá

Keith

Dear Dad, Mam and Michelle

It is now my second day and things are going fine. This is one of the best houses. It is beside, or, down the road from the one I was in last year. Colm is in the worst house and his has been very hungry most of the days. My house is very nice and the people in it are alot of boggers but it is all right. I'm a *kinira* seomra. Its all right. We got here safely and nothing really has happened so there is nothing really to write about. The food is very good and

Mark Scannell (PC) is in my house which is good. There is four chaps in my bed room, all boggers and also there is a wash basin which is very good because I don't have to que.

I have made friends with two fellows or blokes in my house which are quite sound and every thing is brill.

My lip is going down, my five days is up but it wasn't gone so I'm still continueing five times a day. Hopefully it will be gone soon. Renate is very good at being PC again. And Mark also. There is nothing much let to say except I have to walk eight miles a day. So I've got to go. I will write again. My letter has been short. Sorry.

Bye

Keith

From: *Louise Murray*
Age: *13*
Year: *1988*
Home: *Cork*
Gaelteacht: Ceann Trá, Dingle, County Kerry

7 June 1988

Hi Mummy, Daddy agus Susan Phig

Its 10.25 on Tuesday 7 June. The train was quite exhausting and we saw Tim Summers pad from the tracks. Stevie is going to fierce lengths to hide the patch on his pants. He's gone off to O'Donoghues and me to Brid-pats. The rules are strict enough. The lights although have to be out by 11.00. I'm in a room with three other girls from

Dublin, Kerry and Tipperary. They seem sound enough. I had a desperate time trying to fit bags in the bus. I have to be up by 8.15 as opposed to the 11.30-12.00 routine I was used to. My initial impression of Dingle was one of total disgust as one of 'the locals' winked at me. Stephen I think has cheered up a bit and seems to be making friends.

The food (contrary to what you said) is disgusting, strong tea, a slice of tomato, a bit of egg, two slices of lettuce, a ring of onion and a revolting two pieces of Duffys sliced meat. I can now say I would appreciate home-cooking – even if it meant eating gammon-ham (and that's bad!)

I can safely say that I'll be a mere twelve stone (that's about middle weight) on return.

By the way, my bottom brace broke!

Bye for today

Louise

PS I'll have more news tomorrow, on a separate page.

9 June 88
11.11 pm

Yesterday was OK and the *ceilí* was great but I made a mess of the Irish school class this morning because I'm the youngest in the house.

The classes are 10–12.45 but there are two small breaks.

The first paragraph was written yesterday the 9th but I'm going to write the rest of the 9th's happenings today on the 10th at 9.08 am.

Yesterday after the *ceilí* I went for a walk with a boy

and Stephen and his friends. I didn't arrive home till 10.43 and we were meant to be home at 10.30

Una the teacher killed me and I told her I was talking with friends (which I was really). Una said she'd ring my parents and the ard-mhaistir is coming over in a minute to see me.

The food is improving. I don't (even if this blows over) think I can stick the whole three weeks, cause Una hates me now.

PS I'll try and ring ye today and I'll post this letter today. It should get there tomorrow morning the 11th. There's no *ceilí* tomorrow cause there's Mass and there is a class. On Sunday there's no class and a *ceilí*. I don't really like the games cause they don't explain them.

The rooms are lovely! Una will probably ring and even the *bean an tí* said she was fierce strict. I'll try and ring.

Stephen seems to be enjoying himself but I would love to be at home.

I'll send you a postcard soon!

PS The weather is lovely but today's a bit dull.

Bye

Louise

PS If Una rings don't tell her anything. Pretend you don't know anything about it.

How is Susie? Sorry, I just remembered this won't come till Monday!

1.52 pm 10 June 1988

Things have changed since the morning. The *ardmhaistir* came during the boring classes and took me outside. He said it was serious but he only put my name on a piece of paper and if it happens again I'm to go home.

I'd like to go home early you could say I have to get ready for France. I'm going to the village in a minute I'll try and ring.

The *gaelteacht* isn't all its cracked up to be.

It's really the pits here!

From: Kathleen O'Kane
Age: 12
Year: 1988
Home: Dublin
Gaeltacht: Coláiste ne bhFiann, Longford

Coláiste na bhFiann
Coláiste Naoimh Mel
Longphort
16 August 88

Hi Mam and Dad

I hope you are keeping well. I have not got much news. I know what time you have to come up at on Sunday 1.45. Our play was not on Sunday it will be on tonight and I'm a bit nervous but I'm sure it will go great. The man came with all the T-shirts and presents I had £9.00 to spend but then I said to Colm who takes care of the money and the shop that I gave him £7.00 on Sunday. So then I had £16.00. I did not spend it all because I had no time I really feel angry and sad because I wanted to by Mícheal a t-shirt or

some pressent but they give me any time and I also wanted
to buy a packet of earrings they were navey and they would
go nice with my sailor suit. Well I have to go now.
Lots of love
Kathleen
Slán !

From: *Grainne Munnelly*
Age: *15*
Year: *1988*
Home: *Dublin*
Gaeltacht: *Inis Oírr, Aran Islands, County Galway*

[Postcard]

Inish Oírr
Oilean Arainn

Hi
The weather is totally fabulous. I am burned on my face
alot. You would be better to ring in the morning because
we go for walks along the island. The scenery is gorgeous.
I'd say you would love the island. The water is clear like
the Carribean. The rocks are full of ants and crikes and are
quiet dangerous in the part near our house. The weather is
like the postcard nearly everyday but better. The food is
lovely and the island is not the kip Treasa described it to
be. You can see the cliffs of Mohere and Inishméan.
Grainne

From: Stephen Murray
Age: 16
Year: 1988
Home: Cork
Gaeltacht: Ceann Trá, Dingle, County Kerry

Ceann trá

Trá Lí

I Ciarra

Dear Lads

Conas tá sibh? Taím go maith! Everything's fine here.

I'm starting to use Irish here a lot more now. Louise has a boyfriend who's in my house his hame's Kevin, a very sound boy. You must write to me soon. To be allowed smoke around here you have to have parental note and even though I rarely have one it would be great to have in case a teacher questions me. I'm kinda running lowish on money and if you could possibly see your way to forwarding me a bit of money I'd be very grateful. I'm sorry to be writing on a copy page but I've nothing better to use.

In our house we get the best food possible. Everyone else gets just enough. We're always getting treats of lovely food and we never have to do any washing up. She also washes our clothes for us. Do you know that £16 Peter France credit note? Well if your in town go to the rack of 'Fresh Air' shirts in P. France and get me 1 or two because they only cost £8 or something like that. I would like them to be styled or something as far out as possible. If they have Bermuda shorts, get them instead. They have them in great outdoors and if they're cheap would you please get them?

I'll write again soon. I'm terrible for asking for things all the time!

Slán anois.

Say hello to any of my friends for me.

Stephen

PS If you are coming down bring my white jacket please.

From: *Mícheal O'Kane*
Age: *14*
Year: *1988*
Home: *Dublin*
Gaeltacht: *Coláiste na bhFiann, Carlow*

Colaiste na bhFiann
Croc Beag
Ceatharilach
11 August 88

Dia Duit Mam and Dad

I was delighted to receive my first letter. When I opened and found Róisin's letter first I began bursting out laughing thinking that was it you but then I saw your letter. We have started practising our big play at the end of the college. It is very good it is based on the Millenium. There is a Viking called 'Wacker' (from the match boxes) who comes to Ireland for a holiday with his family Hannah his wife, Hector, his son, Caramel who changes her name to

Caremencita Apolls and Fluisey (!) beag. Wacker loves to play golf and Wacker plays a golf match with Brian Boru at Clontarf which ends up in a battle which Wacker wins.

I'm writing this part of the letter on Tuesday 16 August at 12.50 am. I have just received your letter Dad and Cahal's note. I'm fine thank you but very very tired. On Sunday night Malachy Duffin the Irish pop singer came and there was a disco it was brilliant. We were allowed go wild and the *cúinteoirs* were not allowed stop us. They went mad as well.

All the *cúinteoirs* are waiting for their results in the Leaving Cert which comes out tomorrow Wednesday. You can imagine how moody they all are. Tomorrow in the college it is sport all day and guess what? There will be a swimming gala as well. My proud and joy is reaching the semi-final at the table-tennis out of sixty students which I knocked out last year's winner. I play the semi-final today against my best friend in the college Seán who was in Naomh Mel last year. Have to finish off now.

See you on Sunday.

Mícheal xxxxx

PS My arm is OK except a piece of plaster came off where my fingers are. Brendan put it together with Selotape.

From: *Elaine McManamly*
Age: *14*
Year: *1989*
Home: *Dublin*
Gaeltacht: *Camus, County Galway*

Camus

21 July 1989

Hi!

I am just in from my tea, and its 9.30. I just got to the house about an hour ago, it is really nice, there are fourteen of us in it. I am in a room with four others, Clodagh (sixteen), Ciara (fifteen), and Lisa (fourteen). They are nice and are all from Dublin. The *bean an tí* is really nice and the food is georgous, we had chips and burgers for our tea. You won't believe I am in the same house as one of my friends, Olivia, she is in Sarah's class, but I know her through Mairín. I know the *cinnire tí* also she is Barbara's sister Deirdre, she is really nice.

I'd better go now because it is getting late.

Luv

Elaine

PS Please write back soon.

PPS I miss you!!

Hi Mom and Dad!

Just a little note to say things have improved a lot since the last letter, I got your letter yesterday and I got one from Rhonda, and Ciara so I was called up three times,

I was so delighted!

We went on a tour today we went to a swimming pool, then we went to a castle, then to a tower then we went to Spidel and the beach and everyone was in a great mood (including Áine and the teachers) and singing and Áine let us stay up an hour later and get up an hour later, she was in a great mood. In my last letter I really kind of wanted you to come down because I wasn't having a great time and when I am'nt having a great time I think of home and get lonely but it has got much better, so if you can't come I really don't mind, the only reason would be to get out for a while, as well as that a few of my friends are going out with cousins and family.

I'd better go now. I love you!

Elaine.

25 July 1989

Hi!

I am having a good time here, except I am finding it very tiring. We get up at 7.30 in the morning and get dressed and tidy our room, then we have our breakfast and we leave the house at 8.30. We have to walk three miles to the college up and down hills to school. After school we go in a mini bus home and have our dinner around 1.00 then we have free time until around 3.30 then we walk the three miles again to the school for sports, I play volleyball, then at 5.00 we have our tea at the closaiste – we get sandwiches from the *cinnirí tí* and one day we got spam! One day Keith got spam and ketchup mixed together! But yesterday we got turkey. After tea we have a *ceilí* and then around 10.00 we go home and have supper and we have to be in bed with the lights off by 11.00. One of the girls in my bedroom is in love with Conor and can't stop talking about him, and it gets a bit boring at times! Nearly every girl likes him! I am in B class here which is considered good – with Mairin O'Beachain and Gráinne Corbett. There is an A for older people (Conor is in A) B for good, C for younger and allright people and D for people with very little Irish. Paula is in D on her own (without any one she knows) and she doesn't like it, I think she is homesick. In my class we have three different teachers – Liam, Sinéad and Caroline – Liam is the nicest – he does games with us then Sinéad but I don't really like Caroline she talks *really* fast and gets us to do a good bit of work.

The weather has been allright today was the first day of rain. I have to go down for sports now and walk three miles! and post this letter on the way bye!
Elaine
PS Please write back soon.

26 July 1989

Hi

I am having a brilliant time here except I don't really like the classes! But after the classes the day is brilliant. Sorry my letters are so short, but I haven't got much time! I am dying to get a letter! but don't worry I know about the postal strike! It is typical it had to happen at this time. A few of my friends moms and dads are coming this weekend or the weekend after, I would love if you could come, but if you can't I don't mind. I better go now, I miss you!

Bye

Elaine

Hi again!

We have loads of free time today, so I decided to write again. I am having quite a good time here, but it gets a bit boring at times. The weather is cloudy and rainy, not like Dublin! Sometimes I want to go home when it gets boring so do some of my friends, but I don't at the moment, I get lonely sometimes as well! I have a debate in the morning – which I hate, and so does everyone else! I have never even done one in English before, never mind Irish. Its on 'The people of Ireland are lazy' and I am saying they are and I have to talk for two minutes! but the girls in my house are very helpful. Me, Conor, and Sadhbh are going to ask if we can ring, I would love to talk to you and we want to know if you are coming to see us! A good few of my friends moms and dads came this weekend and are coming next! I got your letter on Friday and I was going mad when you were having barbaques and we are all stuck in the rain. Our teachers told us they went to Coláiste Lurgan for a night and there was an awful lot of English being spoken – not like here! I am finding it brilliant from the Irish point of view, I am learning loads of new words and phrases and also songs and *ceilí* dances! Our house is the Camus pony stud. Yesterday one of the horses had a foal and we went to see it, it was gorgeous. Hi, I am just back from dinner, it was gorgeous we had turkey, potatoes carrots, stuffing and gravy, then we had trifle and cream, then tea and biscuits.

We had a sleep-in today (first one too!) We don't have to be at the *Coláiste* until 3.30, but we have to leave the house at 2.30 because it takes us an hour to walk to the *Coláiste*. I better go now! I hope to see you here! I really miss you.
Bye
Luv Elaine

From: *Christabel O'Connor*
Age: *12*
Year: *1989*
Home: *Dublin*
Gaeltacht: *Indreabhán, County Galway*

Indreabhan
County na Gaillimhe
1 July 1989

Dear Guys

    I arrived safely. Dearbhla, Orla and Lorraine are all in the same room as me. There are three other girls Mary/Maire, as we're in the Gaeltacht, Bronagh and Alison. Maire is sort of like our leader. She has just done her Leaving. Her dad is the head-master. Please write back soon. I miss you. In our room there are two bunk beds, a sink, two wardrobes, a locker and a few presses. In the other room there's one bunk and a single bed no sink. On the train the porter told us there were seats up ahead so we squeezed in beside a boy called Alex. He had just come back from Florida and he's going again in October for three years. We

are going to the 'Beat in the Street' tonight. Mam I met
Martin, he's really funny. We're going to the beach in a
minute. The weather is not too bad. There are two *bean an
tí*s. The younger *bean an tí* has two children, one little baby
daughter and a little boy. They make lovely homemade
bread here. Please tell Martin to stop checking on me!
Slán
Chris
Miss you all xxxx

10July 1989
Tuesday 14.44

Dear Mam, Dad and Ben
    Having great fun. Dearbhla and I have little disagree-
ments now and then but everythings fine. I'm missing you,
chips, fruit, fighting with Ben etc. There is a little boy here
called Anya or something he's about four and every time
we have sweets or something he comes into our room and
tries to get some. There is a little baby girl called Nora she
used to be nice until Sunday night but Sunday night she
started crying and screaming which went on for about ten
minutes, constantly! So every time we see her we feel like
killing her. Dearbhla has made friends with Sharon. Sharon
is real nice and she minds Nora and Anya while the younger
bean an tí goes to work and while the older one feeds us
our dinner and sometimes our tea. The younger *bean an tí*
comes back at about 6.15 with the *fear an tí* complecated
eh?
    Anyway today at breakfast we saw about six cows in

the collages garden it was really fun then Helen, the owner of the house, came back and shifted a few of the cows. Later the boys acted as farmers! Yes they got the cows into the field beside us. Then they had to get them out on to the road and in to the other field! Everything was really fun and chaotic.

Answers to your questions

Yes the train was chaos. We did get a seat, the porter told us about seats. Vincent met a friend then two girls called us over and asked us were we for Colaiste Connemara so we went with them. In school we wrote a song about Mairtín Davey to the tune of Cest-ser-ra-ser-ra. Remember Terence! My room has two wardrobes, four presses on top, one locker, two sets of bunks, one sink, blue carpet, mirror, socket and a big mess! Only joking. its got everything except a big mess. We keep our room tidy usually.

Yes I do share with Dearbhla. She sleeps on the top bunk with me below. Please send stamps quickly about 6 24p. I have £20 in the bank and no other money. £10 went for trips £2.50 went for medicine and then I bought postcards. We went into Galway so don't think I spent £30 on sweets. Are you going to come up? Please do. You can stay in the college free, but just bring your own food you can cook it there.

Slan anois (bye now)

Chris xxxxxooo

PS I love you.

PPS Don't be greedy among the kisses!

Colaiste Chonamara
Indreabhan
County Na Gaillimhe
15 June 1990

Dear Mom and Co

Having an OK time! We were going to go into Galway with Lisa's parents but now we have to go to Aran Islands. and I don't want to. *PLease send some money!* I have only £14.83 left and I have to buy prezzies for two girls in my house whose birthday it was a few days ago and your birthday prezzy. I'll write to you later. Mom please stop writing before you hear from me. Send my report. Ring me. if you don't I'll kill you: ring from work! The number I gave you is my house number so just ask for Chris not Christabel because I told the *bean an tí* my name is *Chris* and please don't write Christabel on my letters!!

Sorry about the scribbles out on the other page, I just got your letter a few minutes ago, and I had already started.

Ring me between 1-3pm, 5.10-7pm and 9-11pm any day!

Slán

Chris xxxx

From: *Cathy McGouran*
Age: *13*
Year: *1991*
Home: *Dublin*
Gaeltacht: *Annagry, County Donegal*

Coláiste na Rosann
Anagry
Letterkenny
County Donegal

Yo Julie

Well as promised here is the letter waiting at your doorstep! Guess who is here . . . Rachel Misen, Leslie Kepel and Cathy someone or other. We don't speak any Irish at all!

Not much news since we have only just arrived but we went down to the chipper about an hour ago and met one of the blokes he is fourteen and Clare thinks he fancies me!

Better go now

Bye, Grá

Cathy

Coláiste na Rosann
9 August 1991

Julie!

Hope you enjoyed France. I am writing to you again 'cause I have nothing else to do!!! (only kidding!) Notice the date. I will be fourteen in exactly two months. You can start

109

thinking about a present!!! (only kidding again!!)

I *do not* and I repeat *do not* fancy Johnathon Cook. Clare won £19 in the £3,000,000 Jackpot 'cause we all did a ticket. I got 1 number [six]. Clare also lost two pairs of socks. I will now tell you about the people in this house.

Nina: very nice, mad into football (seventeen: oldest)

Mary: mad crack, really nice, looks like you. (seventeen) looks thirteen.

Mairead: never stops laughing, intends bumping into me in a posh hotel when Clare is teaching me how to eat (sixteen)

Angie: very nice, has gourgus naturally curly hair (sixteen)

Gillian: a bit of a loner, not well liked (sixteen)

Tara: mad crack, never stops talking and saying marvelous/mercyful hour, classic (fifteen)

Pauline: the smallest, good crack (fifteen)

Verona: nice, bit moody (fifteen) Nina's sister.

Lisa: nice, bit moody (fifteen)

Pamela: mad crack, lives in Tallagh (fourteen)

Zelie: mad crack, Pamela's friend also lives in Tallaght (fourteen)

Carlin: Pauline's sister. very nice (fourteen)

Siobhán: really, really, friendly (fourteen)

Marion: very nice (thirteen)

Clare: (fourteen) what else can I say?

Me: (thirteen) the youngest and coolest.

Well that's it for now. Don't forget to write you lazy bitch.
Cathy

110

Coláiste na Rossan
Anagary
Letterkenny
County Donegal
13 August1991

Yo Julie

Well I'm just off the phone about a half an hour but since you love getting letters here you go!

I have decided to tell you all we have done so far – so here goes . . .

Tuesday 30 July

Arrived in Anagary at 6.00 pm. Had the evening off.

Wednesday 31 July

Went to school, got sorted into classes. Climbed a small mountain, had a disco.

Thursday 1 August

Went to school, learnt how to *ceilí* dance, had *ceilí* and disco.

Friday 2 August

Went to school, went crab fishing, had treasure hunt.

Saturday 3 August

School, went to beach, played sports.

Sunday 4 August

Mass (9 am–Irish), Arts and Crafts, ceilí and disco.

Monday 5 August

School, climbed Mount Errigal (third highest mountain in Ireland), disco.

Tuesday 6 August

School, went to beach, played sports.

Wednesday 7 August

School, went to Dunlevy, Ceilí and Disco.

Thursday 8 August

School, big long walk, ceilí and disco.

Friday 9 August

School, bingo, ceilí.

Saturday 10 August

School, shopping in Dunlow, Treasure hunt.

Sunday 11 August

Mass (9 am-Irish), Board games, ceilí and disco.

Monday 12 August

School, played sports, had table quiz.

Tuesday 13 August

School, watched *Three Men and a Little Lady*, fancy dress, ceilí and disco.

Well that is all of the news up until now so I will put together a typical day for you. Take for example yesterday 12 August . . .

8.30 am   Half the house gets up and queues for the bathroom.

9.00 am   *Bean an tí* says breakfast is ready and the other half (including me) gets up and scrambles to the breakfast table.

9.30 am   Brekfast is over people go back to bed or get dressed.

9.50 am   Maad rush to get ready and out of the house.

10.00 am   Classes

11.00 am   Break – everybody goes to the shop.

11.20 am   Classes

12.15 pm   Singing (mad crack).

12.45 pm   Post is given out.

12.50 pm   Go home for lunch/dinner.

1.00 pm–3.00 pm   Mess around Anagary

3.00 pm   Back to the Collage and up to the primary school for sports. esterday we had an obstical course, I fell and ripped a hole in the knee of my trousers and cut my knee and played basketball.

5.00 pm   Back home for tea. Free till 8 pm.

8.00 pm   Ceilí at the College.

9.00 pm   Disco at the College.

10.00 pm   Free till 10.30 pm. Usually everybody goes to Dino's (chipper). The one and only Anagary hangout spot.

10.30 pm   Home for supper.

11.30 pm   Lights out (we usually talk for hours).

Earley Hours of Morning: We finally fall asleep.

I will now explain Anagary to you . . .

Anagary is one long street. There are two grocery shops. The Cope and Mace and a sweet shop. Dino's the chipper is where everybody hangs out. There is a phone box there where I make my calls. There is a Catholic church and a graveyard. There are loads of B & Bs and of course the Coláiste!!

Well, I think I've written enough for now, since you always say I write such short letters!

Bye for now

Love and stuff

Cathy

PS Say hi to everybody for me and say I'm enjoying myself.

Coláiste na Rossan
Anagary
Letterkenny
County Donegal
13 August1991

Hi, it's me again

We had a fancy-dress *ceilí* and disco tonight. It was great fun. I was dressed as a hippy! It was maad crack. Mairead in our house dressed up as a curehead-spool. The three Belfast lads (actually one is Scottish) dressed up as girls two of them even got bras!. Another bloke Fionn also dressed up as a girl.

If you remember today on the phone I was telling you about Flick and Spike (the two Fergals) and Colm. Well I have just been told to tell you that the five other girls in my room fancy Flick. I do too and Colm also. They are un-be-leve-able.

Well life is cool,
Bye for now.
Love and stuff
Cathy
PS Sorry this letter isn't very long.
PPS I don't think Rachel Misson is going with Paul (from Belfast).

Coláiste na Rossan
Anagary
Letterkenny
County Donegal
14 August1991

Dia dhuit, an bhfuil tú go maith?
Hi ya!

Mise arís (me again!!) you are probably sick of getting letters from me by now, but what the heck! Life is great, people are great, I'm great! (ha, ha) A bit of news to tell you that I forgot to . . .

Two blokes had a punch-up the other day – one ended up with a black eye and the other with a broken fist! They got into dead shit.

About a week ago I was in class with a girl called Arelene when she started getting really bad pains in her tummy. At first she thought it was just cramps so the nurse (who calls every day) sent her to bed. They weren't getting better at all and she couldn't even stand up straight. The doctor came and said it was her appendix so he rushed her into hospital in Letterkenny in an ambulance. She got her appendix out and will not be coming back. She was really nice. I must write to her when I finish this fifth letter to you.

My friend Tara (the maaad one) will enclose a letter to you.

Everyone here says hi (except Clare who is in a very strange mood!)

Hope you enjoyed my fifth letter, don't expect any

more 'cause I'm running out of stamps!!

Bye

See ya when I get back,

Love 'n' stuff! (hope you don't mind me stealing your phrase)

Cathy.

PS Say hi to everyone for me.

PPS If you want any more letters send me stamps (just kidding!)

PPS Tara's Johnathan Cook joke is a very big joke!

> Coláiste na Rosann
> Anagry
> Letterkenny
> County Donegal
> 19 August1991

Hello Julie,

Hows life. Thanks for your other letter. Here is another to amaze your mother! I'm still having a great time, but tomorrow is my last day and on Wednesday we are all going home, by the way I'll ring you on Wednesday. Now for the big news . . . I'm in love. Well I fancy Colm Rafferty. He lives in Clonskeagh but I don't think he fancies me. In fact he is cracked into somebody else. He is fifteen, a bit chubby wears a brace and is very cute and very friendly. Mary, who is going with Mick, said it to him last night. I still haven't a clue what is going on.

Well bye for now.

Keep smiling.

Love n' stuff
Cathy
PS Tara encloses another letter!
PPS Mairead says Hi.

[Post card from Anagary]
Hello again! I'm writing to you in the middle of signing. I
hope you like the card. It's an old one of Anagary. We had
to buy one for a treasure hunt we did the other night. You
will probably be wondering why I am writing you so many
letters. Well the reason is . . . I like writing them and you
like getting them. Well *slán go foill,*
Love and stuff
Cathy
PS Say hi to everybody for me.

From:	*Brian Farrell*
Age:	*11*
Year:	*1993/1994*
Home:	*Dublin*
Gaeltacht:	*Coláiste Lurgan*

Col Lurgan

Hi Mam and Dad
How are you. I am fine. I feel a little bit weird writing this
letter to you in English because I am now so used to people
talking in Irish. People have been caught speaking English
but were not sent home. I was very nervous the first day

but now have settled down. I am writing this letter to you in bits and three people have been sent home. I miss you alot and can't wait to see you this weekend.

Slán

Brian

To Mam and Dad

How are you. Did you enjoy your holiday. Well I am enjoying mine. I went to the beach today like I do every sunny day. Sorry about the card but it was the last one in the shop and they were not getting any more in until Wednesday. But happy birthday Dad and have a nice time and Darragh did you have a nice time in Wexford. Did you like the Harwoods. So I have to go see you on Sunday.

Love

Brian

Col. Lurgan

7 July 94

Hello!

Brian here for a few words. So how are you Mam & Dad Fiona and Darragh. I am great. My *bean an tí* is nice and in our spare time we can play football and basket ball. My *kinnera* is sound they are thirteen in my house. We had a *ceile* on Friday. *Tá mo calíní ag damsa le mise go dheas.* (Just thought I'd say that). So is the window fixed yet. Tell Darragh not to worry it could of happened to anybody. So send down thirty pounds

I am now writing on Wednesday the 7th. Because when

I was writing first the *bean an tí* came in and said turn off the light and I had to. I am in rang Banba. I went canoeing two days ago. It was freezing. Well Mam I better go.
So bye love ye and leave ye.
Slán
Brian

From: *Jane Kelly*
Age: *12*
Year: *1994*
Home: *Cork*
Gaeltacht: *Coláiste Íde, Dingle, County Kerry*

Colaíste Ide
Tralee
6 July 1994

Dear Parents
If you bring me home, I am willing to pay for the remaining two weeks of this course. You can stop my pocket money. I'll go without new clothes for the rest of my childhood. I'll live on Anne's castoffs. I'll live on Anne's leftovers! (That's what we have to do here). Please take me home now, I can't stand much more of this. It isn't even *fun*. We don't get to go to the beach or Dingle and games is torture.

I really mean it, Anne, even if I do get over this homesickness, I'll never enjoy it. The teachers aren't even sympathetic, they're hard and cruel. I'm sick of being called 'Síne' also. I won't learn much Irish because no-one speaks

119

it and I was put in a duff class because I never came down here before. I swear I'll get out my *Jimín* and teach myself. I'll do a dozen book reviews! I'll try and stick it out the first week till you come at the weekend (meaning Saturday at the latest) *to take me home*. But, if I *can't* bear it that long, I'll ring you, OK? So glad you agree! Can't wait! Looking forward!

Miss you!

Jane xxxooo

PS Oh yes! And I'll do all the housework you want me to.

PPS Please! You don' realise. I'm not cut out for this! DON'T ignore me. Don't(!) Don't(!) ignore me!!!

PPPS I'll go to Micromail every day or Oyster Haven and I'll invite people over! I love you both.

PPPS I'm sorry to be such a dissapointment as a daughter. I know I've done this so many times before. Please don't give me a hard time over this! It's the way I am! The way I *feel!* At least take my offer into considerationbut *don't ignore* it.

46 Naoim Pádraig

Coláiste Íde

Tralee

Oiche Dé Deárdaoin

7 Iúil 94

Parents

I do not want to upset you, but truly I wish to go home. My Irish *has* improved. Even last night someone said I was talking in my sleep. Please say that's enough! I can't write properly in this light, I'll continue this tomorrow.

Oh No! Three weeks of this! Torture! Oh for home! Home, where I can answer the phone and not queue for it. Home, with a full-length mirror in my bedroom. Personally, I think one week is enough, thank you very much. I know I did this in Murphy's Farm and tried it in Oyster Haven. I don't think I'm ready for the Gaiety, I'd miss home too much. Can't wait to see you both on Sunday. Kindly consider taking me home then. I'm sorry to hear Lulu's on crutches. What if she never walks again? I'd like to be home for the bad news, not here. Thank you for the petal, Anne.

Jane

PS Had to keep it short, bell rang.

From:	*Joanna Connell*
Age:	*14*
Year:	*1995*
Home:	*Cork*
Gaeltacht:	*Muiríoch, Dingle, County Kerry*

Hi Noreen

How are you? Everything is brilliant down here. I don't particularly like classes because they're boring. *Tá bucaillí go hálínn are fad* well four good looking. Well, bye for now.

See you soon.

Lots of Luv

Joanna

Joanne luvs Philip 4 ever

From: *Barry Doyle*
Age: *12*
Year: *1995*
Home: *Dublin*
Gaeltacht: *Ballinskelligs, County Kerry*

Colaiste Mhichíl
Baile 'n Sceilig
Contae Chiarraí
July 1995

Dear Mum and Dad

This is me, Barry, I have just finished my first full day at the Gailtact. The *kalie* was *brilliant* and guess what a girl asked to to dance. Yes that's right, she asked *me*!

Earlier on yesterday we went swimming in the sea which was quite warm which didn't surprise me one bit considering the weather which is uncomfortably hot. Every morning I have to cycle one and a quarter miles to the college, then back again for dinner. Walking, the trip takes about forty minutes. For dinner I had beef carrots and potatoe. The most amazing thing about this place is the amount of tea you're expected to drink.

There's no cardphone so my phone card is useless. I'm having a great time but I don't wish you were here so don't visit.

Love

Barry Doyle

From: Simon Boland
Age: 12
Year: 1995
Home: Dublin.
Gaeltacht Colaiste Mhichíl, Baile 'n Sceilig, Contae
             Chiarraí

[July 95]

Dear Mom and Dad

This letter is for the both of you, so you can sort this out yourselves. OK, well let's see now. Oh, by the way I haven't put the address at the top because I don't know it and there's really no point in writing back . . . on my point of view. About the 'College', to be honest I don't know what I think of it cause I only arrived yesterday. Our 'Banóntí (I cant spell it so don't tease me about it when I get back, you hear) is sort of soft and is very easy to bribe. The place is fine exept it's a mile and a half away from the village. But you know that, don't you?

Not much Irish spoken I'm afraid; we're all trying though, don't worry. The girls are nice, but all about fifteen or so. I've got £55 left, and I get the bike to school. I went for a swim today. It was like swimming in paradise with the warm, clear water and the golden sand all over the beach. But there's dog shit everywhere and annoying little midgets flying around eating your head. By the way I'm sorry about the first page. It got, never mind. I havn't done the *kaylees* yet. I'm doing them tonight.

I'll see if I can find a telephone for callcards or else

123

just use the pay phone. I'll think about writing back, so in the meantime, forget about me!

Goodbye!

Dear Mother and Father

I hate to tell you this but I'm not really learning as much Irish as you expected. I've got £25 left and today is 13.7.95. So I've got more money than I should have. We're all going to the Aquadome in Tralee. I'm thinking of getting my hair cut and honestly don't give a ... what the pair of you think. It's my hair after all. You should see my hair it's like a ... jungle. The girl I like, 'Máire', she gave me a crossbar on my bike the other day. I asked her where she was from and she said 'Killarney'.

You know I have to pay £6 for the trip. £6. Well I guess it's not so bad cause I've already paid it.

The reason I haven't been ringing much is that there isn't a cardphone anywhere apart from the one half way up Bolus Head in 'Cille Rillege' or something. Well, I guess that's it then.

Goodbye

Simon

[Opposite is picture by Simon Boland.]

From: *Susan Murray*
Age: *14*
Year: *1995*
Home: *Cork*
Gaeltacht: *Muiríoch, Dingle County Kerry*

10 June 1995

Dear Mum,

I am having a mad time. We are learning loads of Irish and smoking lots of hash and drinking. (*not*) What ever you do, Mom, don't come down, please.

We hang around with loads of boys and everyone is mad cause they are the best looking. Any gossip? Please get a dog. We are right next to the hall, the shops and the beach. It's past my bed time so

Bye

Susan Murray

16 June 95

Dear Mam,

The weather has drastickly deteroriated. I have got a really good tan on my tummy and on my arms and face. I'm eating loads of food even though the woman is not a very good cook. I am writing on my bed at the moment.

Joanne shifted one of the locals, his name is Stephen. We hang around with the Limerick girls in our room Marita Mi and Audrey they are all sound and easy to get along with.

On the three glorious days we had we went swimming and sunbathed on the beach. We are all planning to gaff out on the last night and some of my friends' *bean an tí* said that they were leaving the doors open. I have not watched any TV since we arrived.

Love you

Susan Clare Murray

Dear Louise

How's it going? I miss home and my friends a bit but it's mad down here so it's OK. No guys my type down here (too small). One of the locals likes me! Well, he used to a few days ago – don't know about now.

Loads of Cork people down here, it's a mady.

I have lots of gossip to tell you when I get home.

Love you

Suz

——————————————————